THE LIES WE BELIEVE

WORKBOOK

DR. CHRIS THURMAN

A JANET THOMA BOOK

THOMAS NELSON PUBLISHERS
Nashville • Atlanta • London • Vancouver

Published in Nashville, Tennessee, by Thomas Nelson, Inc., Publishers, and
distributed in Canada by Word Communications, Ltd., Richmond, British
Columbia.

Unless otherwise noted the Bible version used in this publication is THE
NEW KING JAMES VERSION. Copyright © 1979, 1980, 1982, 1990, Thomas
Nelson, Inc., Publishers.

Scripture quotations marked NIV are taken from The Holy Bible: New
International Version. Copyright © 1973, 1978, 1984 by the International
Bible Society. Used by permission of Zondervan Bible Publishers.

ISBN 0-7852-8087-1

Printed in the United States of America.

1 2 3 4 5 6 — 00 99 98 97 96 95

CONTENTS

Acknowledgments   *v*

1. The Ultimate War: Lies Versus Truth   *1*

2. Developing the Mind of Christ: The TRUTH System   *13*

3. Defeating Self Lies   *33*

4. Defeating Worldly Lies   *65*

5. Defeating Marital Lies   *91*

6. Defeating Distortion Lies   *115*

7. Defeating Religious Lies   *139*

8. The Truths We Must Believe for Emotional Health: Part One   *163*

9. The Truths We Must Believe for Emotional Health: Part Two   *191*

10. The Truth About God   *213*

11. The Truth About You   *235*

12. Pressing on to the Mind of Christ   *261*

ACKNOWLEDGMENTS

It has been five years since I wrote *The Lies We Believe*. As a nervous and pessimistic first-time author, I prayed that at least ten copies of my book would be sold (members of my family assured me that they would buy a total of eight copies, so I felt reasonably sure that my goal was within reach). I had no idea that more than 100,000 copies of *The Lies We Believe* would be sold or that the book would allow me to travel around the country doing a seminar by the same name that thousands have attended. God has blessed the book and the seminar beyond my wildest dreams.

People who attend my seminar are always gracious in their comments about how they have been helped by *The Lies We Believe*—music to my ears, to be sure. The one question I am asked everywhere I go is "Why don't you do a workbook that will take us step by step through your book and make it easier to put what you teach into practice?" Well, I am delighted to respond to that question with what you now hold in your hands. I hope those of you who wanted this workbook will feel that it was worth the wait.

I have many people to thank for their help. Bill Butterworth took my writings and seminar lectures and turned them into the many questions and assignments in this workbook. He did a fantastic job, and I am deeply grateful for all of his hard work. Janet Thoma, as usual, was an important source of encouragement during this project. Her support of my writing efforts over the years has been invaluable. My wife, Holly, and my children,

Matthew, Ashley, and Kelly, are all that any man could ask for. They help keep my emotional gas tank full so that I can devote myself to projects such as this one. Finally, and most important, I thank God for making His home in my heart and for allowing me the privilege of counseling, writing, and doing seminars. I am amazed that He loves someone like me, much less that He uses me to help others.

The apostle Paul, writing almost two thousand years ago, said, "For the time will come when men will not put up with sound doctrine. Instead, to suit their own desires, they will gather around them a great number of teachers to say what their itching ears want to hear. They will turn their ears away from the truth and turn aside to myths" (2 Tim. 4:3–4 NIV). I believe the time Paul was warning us about has come. We are bombarded every day with distortions, half-truths, and outright lies being passed off as truth. There has never been a more important time for each of us to face the lies we have chosen to believe and to devote ourselves to their destruction. We must commit ourselves to truth no matter what the cost may be. Our emotional health and spiritual maturity hang in the balance.

I pray that God will use this workbook to help you find the maturity and the freedom that are available to all who seek Him. May God bless.

Dr. Chris Thurman
Austin, Texas
August, 1994

Chapter 1

THE ULTIMATE WAR: LIES VERSUS TRUTH

On October 31, 1938, Americans across the country were going about their normal routines, until a radio broadcast sent much of the nation into a tailspin.

That Halloween evening, Orson Welles broadcast his version of the H. G. Wells classic, *The War of the Worlds*.

The story describes a Martian invasion of New Jersey. Tuning in too late to hear the announcer introduce the piece as science fiction, people all over the country took the broadcast for fact, believing Martians really had invaded the country! Frightened men, women, and children created mass panic that evening. Some people even attempted suicide, choosing to take their lives rather than face enemy aliens.

Orson Welles helped create tumult in the United States that October evening, but more specifically, individuals panicked because of what they chose to believe.

We are facing an invasion today that, unlike the fictional Martian invasion in *The War of the Worlds,* is quite real. It is an invasion of lies. Lies have invaded our minds and are wreaking havoc on our lives. They are destroying our emotional health, our relationships, our work lives, our families, and our faith. Some people even choose to end their lives because of these lies.

All of us have chosen to believe certain lies, and we are paying an extremely high price for doing so. We, like many people on the night of October 31, 1938, have sent our lives into a frightening tailspin because we have believed lies rather than the truth. It would appear that lies are winning and that the casualty list is growing by the hour.

Do you want to quit believing lies and stop the emotional and spiritual damage they cause? If you do, this workbook is for you.

YOUR MENTAL TAPE DECK

Your brain is like a tape deck. It can record and play back, and it has access to a personal library of thousands of tapes ready to play at a moment's notice. These tapes hold all beliefs, attitudes, and expectations that you've "recorded" during your life.

Some of the tapes inside your brain are truthful, such as "You can't please everybody all the time" or "Life is sometimes rough." Some of these tapes are lies, such as "I'm only as good as what I do" or "Life should be fair" or "Things have to go my way for me to be happy." These tapes dramatically impact your feelings and actions each day. Your emotional and spiritual health hinge on these tapes since they are a direct reflection of whether your mind is controlled by lies or truth.

We cannot always control circumstances, but with help and hard work, we can control our thoughts. Our primary focus in life, then, should not be on changing the circumstances surrounding us, although there is nothing wrong with improving them when we can. A much more important challenge in life is to make our mental tapes as truthful as possible so we can maturely handle whatever circumstances come our way.

Lies produce emotional misery.

Truth produces emotional health.

It's as simple as that.

WHAT ARE YOUR LIES?

Are you wondering what your lies are? Take a minute to complete the following self-analysis questionnaire to find out. Read each statement and indicate your agreement/disagreement with it using the following scale:

1	2	3	4	5	6	7
strongly disagree			neutral			strongly agree

Do not spend too much time on any one statement, but give the answer that best describes how you *really* feel. Try to avoid using the neutral (4) response.

_____ 1. I must be perfect.

_____ 2. I must have everyone's love and approval.

_____ 3. It is easier to avoid problems than to face them.

_____ 4. Things have to go my way for me to be happy.

_____ 5. My unhappiness is externally caused.

_____ 6. I can have it all.

_____ 7. I am only as good as what I do.

_____ 8. Life should be easy.

_____ 9. Life should be fair.

_____ 10. I shouldn't have to wait for what I want.

_____ 11. People are basically good.

_____ 12. My marriage problems are my spouse's fault.

_____ 13. If my marriage takes hard work, my spouse and I must not be right for each other.

_____ 14. My spouse should meet all my needs.

_____ 15. My spouse owes me for what I have done for him/her.

_____ 16. I shouldn't have to change who I am in order to make my marriage better.

_____ 17. My spouse should be like me.

_____ 18. I often make mountains out of molehills.

_____ 19. I often take things personally.

_____ 20. Things are black and white to me.

_____ 21. I often miss the forest for the trees.

_____ 22. The past predicts the future.

_____ 23. I often reason things out with my feelings rather than the facts.

_____ 24. God's love can be earned.

_____ 25. God hates the sin and the sinner.

_____ 26. Because I'm a Christian, God will protect me from pain and suffering.

_____ 27. All of my problems are caused by my sins.

_____ 28. It is my Christian duty to meet all the needs of others.

_____ 29. Painful emotions such as anger, depression, and anxiety are signs that my faith in God is weak.

_____ 30. God can't use me unless I am spiritually strong.

Each of the statements in the list is a lie or a way that we lie to ourselves. Thus, the more you agreed with each statement, the more you are agreeing with a lie. Go back through your responses and put a check mark by any statement that you marked with a (5), (6), or (7). Those are the lies that you tend to

_____

believe the most and the ones you want to pay the most attention to as you interact with this workbook.

USING THIS WORKBOOK

The most effective way to use this workbook is to start at the beginning and work through it carefully to the end. Each chapter is important, and each one builds on the others. Since this is a workbook, it is made up predominantly of exercises requiring your personal interaction. You'll quickly discover you enjoy certain types of assignments better than others. Try to give equal importance to all of them, however. Also, don't allow any of the exercises to intimidate you or make you feel stupid, since a workbook is not able to give you the helpful feedback a person would. Some people will choose to do this book in the context of a group so they can have someone—whether it be a counselor, a friend, or support group members—with whom to discuss some of their questions, thoughts, and feelings.

This workbook is only as helpful as you make it. Give yourself permission to open up freely—perhaps interacting with aspects of your life you've previously kept hidden. Remember, no one is looking over your shoulder, no one is critiquing you, no one is giving you a grade. Just be honest.

Keep your workbook in a safe place. It is vital for you to feel that your thoughts and feelings will remain private. You may want to share some of this material with other people, but you should be able to determine when and how much.

Make a commitment to work regularly in this book, just as if you were keeping a business appointment. Choose a time when you can work at a relaxed pace without being interrupted. Mark it down in your date book.

When will you schedule time to work in this book?

Day of the week: _____

Time of the day: _____

Where you work is also important. Choose a setting that is comfortable, and free from distractions.

Where will you work on your workbook? _____

THE ULTIMATE SOURCE OF TRUTH

What is truth? At the risk of making a classic understatement, I define truth as reality as it is, not as it seems to be. Can we know the unvarnished truth of a situation? Yes, but knowing and understanding the truth are skills that have to be learned, and as with most skills, learning them can be quite difficult and painful at times. Yet the more you practice, the better you get. The better you get, the healthier you become. The more you are able to see truth about yourself and life, the more you'll be able to see past your lies' smokescreens, and that is one of the skills this workbook can help you develop.

I want to add one important caveat about truth. I believe that certain truths, "ultimate truths" that give focus and meaning and substance to life, can be learned only through spiritual means. Truth is like an iceberg. What we can learn from our everyday experiences is just the tip of truth that we can learn on our own. Knowing the deeper, spiritual truths that lie below life's surface requires that we depend on a power greater than ourselves. It seems planned that way. To learn truths that are most powerful and life-sustaining, we must look to God and His Word.

I hope you have a Bible and that you are prepared to use it

as the foundational source to this workbook. Let's begin by turning to Proverbs 23:7.

For as he thinks in his heart, so is he.

Take a minute to let those words sink in. Don't allow their simplicity to betray their depth. What does that verse really say? Rewrite the verse in your own words, emphasizing what you feel is most important.

_____

_____

How does this verse relate to your mental tape deck?

_____

_____

Let's pursue this thought further. Turn to the New Testament, specifically to Philippians 2:5.

Your attitude should be the same as that of Christ Jesus (NIV).

What attitudes come to mind when you think of Christ? List up to eight that you consider the most important.

1. _____
2. _____
3. _____
4. _____
5. _____
6. _____
7. _____
8. _____

Look over your list and pick two of Christ's attitudes that you see in your life. Write down a specific way you display each attitude in your life.

1. I see the attitude of _____ in my life. I display it by

_____

_____

_____

2. I also see the attitude of _____ in my life. I display it by

_____

_____

_____

Look at Colossians 3:2:

Set your minds on things above, not on earthly things (NIV).

What do you think the apostle Paul meant by "things above"?

_____

_____

Look back at the self-analysis questionnaire on pages 3–4. Would you say it represents "things above" or "earthly things"?

_____

Let's look at one more verse of Scripture, Romans 12:2.

Do not conform any longer to the pattern of this world, but be transformed by the renewing of your mind. Then you will be able to test and approve what God's will is—his good, pleasing and perfect will (NIV).

This verse is absolutely critical to the entire process of learning to replace lies with the truth, and by doing so, enjoying the health and well-being we're seeking.

Read the verse again, and circle the words you consider to be key.

Now, rewrite the verse in your own words. (This is called *paraphrasing,* and it is a beneficial way to interact with Scripture because it personalizes it.)

_____

_____

_____

_____

What lies have you bought into that have caused you to be conformed to this world?

_____

_____

In very practical terms, how do you renew your mind?

_____

_____

What role does the Bible play in how you think, since it is the ultimate written source of truth?

_____

_____

_____

LOOKING OVER
WHERE WE'VE BEEN

We've covered a lot of ground already in this workbook. At the conclusion of each chapter, you'll find space for a personal review of what you learned. To facilitate your thinking for this review, I'd like you to write a letter—to yourself! In this letter, I'd like you to be quite candid about your discoveries. What did you learn about lies in general? Specifically, what lies have you been telling yourself? What impact did the self-analysis questionnaire have on you? And what about the Scripture verses we studied? What did you come away with in terms of truth for your life? As you write this letter, try to balance the truth you learned with how you can put it into practice in your life. Write as much as you can. The purpose of this exercise is to summarize and solidify this material. Go for it!

Dear _____ ,

_____

_____

_____

_____

_____

_____

_____

_____

_____

_____

Signed, _____

GROUP DISCUSSION STARTERS

Although this workbook is designed for personal study, I know some of you will use it in the context of a discussion group. Therefore, I want to end each chapter with some optional discussion starters, in case you need help "jump-starting" your discussions.

If you are in a discussion group, try to avoid the two extremes in discussion. If you are a real talker, resist the temptation to talk so much that you dominate the group. If you tend to be quiet, make sure you speak up at regular intervals. Be sensitive to one another, allowing each person to have a chance to speak. If someone doesn't care to speak, that's okay, too. Just be aware.

If your group is made up of an even number of people, each person may want to pick a "buddy" in the group to be especially sensitive to during discussion times. Look out for each other, and be available to talk together, pray together, or whatever. If you are in a group with your spouse, you may want to pick him/her, or you may prefer to pick a buddy of your same sex.

1. Have you ever witnessed or been in a situation similar to the one caused by the Orson Welles radio broadcast? Share with the group what took place and how you felt.

2. Can you identify with the analogy of the mental tape deck? Share with the group one of the most significant tapes you "recorded" while growing up—be it true or false.

3. When you took the self-analysis questionnaire, how did you do? Did you score better or worse than you expected? What, if anything, surprised you about the test?

4. Of the thirty statements in the questionnaire, which ones had particular meaning to you and why?

5. Did one of the Scripture verses in this chapter stand out to you? Why? What did you learn through studying these verses?

6. Based on what you learned in this chapter, respond to this statement: *Believing lies causes significant emotional and spiritual damage, and believing truth is the only path to emotional and spiritual health and the freedom Christ came to offer us.*

Chapter 2

Developing the Mind of Christ: The Truth System

My friend Charlie loves to recount the story of the weekend his wife was sick and bedridden and he was in charge of their four children, all under age ten.

According to Charlie, Saturday went okay, but everyone knew the real pressure would be on Sunday. "Will Daddy dare try to take us to church?" the kids mused. This was a gutsy assignment for a rookie, but to his credit, Charlie was up for the challenge.

He awoke Sunday morning much earlier than usual. He fed his kids a hot breakfast (thanks to microwavable waffles), sent them off one by one to the bathtub to "de-syrup" their sticky bodies, supervised their dressing in their Sunday best, and loaded them in the car for their journey to church.

When they arrived at church, the older children assisted their younger siblings to their Sunday school classrooms while Charlie went to "big church." Getting the children to church without help from his wife was quite an accomplishment, and Charlie was understandably proud.

But, as we all know, pride goes before a fall.

When church concluded, Charlie hung around to fellowship with other church members. Actually, Charlie hung around to brag to his friends about what he had accomplished that morning. He got a little carried away, and a fair amount of time passed.

When he glanced at his watch, he realized his kids would be waiting for him at the car, so he hustled to the parking lot.

He was met with a chorus from the kids, "Dad, where have you been? Let's go! We're ready to go home!"

As the kids piled into the car, Charlie still felt good. He'd done it. He'd pulled it off without a hitch. They pulled into the driveway, and Charlie wanted to be the first to tell his wife about his success.

It was while he was describing his success to his wife that their oldest child politely knocked on the bedroom door and asked, "Dad, have you seen Debbie?"

Debbie was Charlie's eight-year-old daughter, and nobody could find her. No one had seen her since church. At that moment Charlie realized he hadn't seen her in the car on the way home from church!

Embarrassed beyond belief, Charlie sped to church to find his daughter safely waiting with a family who just minutes before was listening to Charlie brag about his Super Dad status. Debbie was fine, but it took Charlie a long time to live that one down.

What sort of feelings run through your mind when you read the story of Charlie's oversight? Since no one was in any real danger, do you find the story humorous? Or do you think to yourself, *How could any responsible adult be so careless?*

An insightful way to look at this story is to put yourself in Charlie's shoes. How would you feel if you left your kid behind?

What would it be like for you to return to church after you discovered your mistake? What sort of things would you say to yourself on the ride from home to church? Unfortunately, many of us would be screaming inside, *What a stupid idiot I am. What kind of moron leaves his daughter at church without realizing it? Incredible! Now everyone will think I'm really wacko. I'm a real jerk!*

Okay, so you made a mistake. But do you see the lies we tell ourselves? Making a mistake is a lot different from being a stupid idiot, moron, wacko, jerk.

In this chapter, I want to introduce you to a model that will help you better understand what lies you believe, the damage those lies cause, and the power of truth to set you free from that damage.

THE TRUTH SYSTEM

What would ultimately help Charlie successfully handle what he did and how he felt about it, is a helpful exercise that can be beneficial to you, too.

The exercise involves using what I call the TRUTH system. Each letter in the acronym, *TRUTH*, stands for an important issue in your effort to achieve emotional and spiritual maturity. Let me briefly introduce this system to you.

The first *T* stands for *trigger event*. This is an event or situation that happens to you. For example, you might be at a movie and someone behind you might start talking too loudly. Or you might be rushing to get to an appointment and accidentally lock your keys in your car. Or, on a more serious level, you might be fired from your job or perhaps informed of the sudden, unexpected death of a loved one.

The *R* stands for *reckless thinking*. This is the time you spend thinking about what has just happened and is often referred to as "self talk." If you locked your keys inside the car, you might think something like, *I am really a stupid fool. What kind of idiot locks his keys in his car at a time like this? Now I'll miss my appointment and everybody will be mad at me. What a moron I am!* We call this self talk "reckless" thinking because our initial thoughts about many trigger events are often faulty (irrational, unrealistic, distorted) and lead to damaging emotional and behavioral consequences.

The *U* stands for *unhealthy response*. These responses are the unhealthy physiological, emotional, and behavioral reactions to the trigger event and your faulty thinking about it. These are unnecessarily painful and unproductive. For example, when you become overly frustrated and angry about the car keys, your physiological reaction will probably be an increased heart rate, muscle tension, and shortness of breath. Your emotional reaction might be a combination of heightened anger and anxiety. Your behaviorial reaction might be that you kick the car door and pound the hood. All these reactions hurt you, and they don't get your keys out of the car.

The second *T* stands for *truthful thinking*. At this point you need to make yourself face the truth about the trigger event. For example, the truth is everyone makes mistakes—to err is human. So, as you stand outside your car, you might say, "Okay, this is inconvenient, but I'm not the first person to lock his keys in his car. This doesn't make me an idiot. I'm not happy about it, but it's not the end of the world. If people get mad at me for being late, I'll tell them exactly what happened. No doubt they've done the same thing." The primary emphasis here is on telling yourself the truth to fight the lies and distortions you told yourself at the reckless thinking stage.

Finally, the *H* stands for *healthy response*. After telling yourself the truth, you should react in a healthier manner than you did during the reckless thinking stage. For example, after telling yourself the truth about locking your keys in the car, you may become less angry and more calm, and move to find help so you can resolve your dilemma.

Initially, you may tell yourself the truth and remain just as upset as you were to begin with. Don't get discouraged. This only means that the faulty and erroneous thoughts you had during the reckless thinking stage were extremely deep and well rehearsed. It will take some time and hard work before you will be able to replace such self-destructive thoughts—lies—with the truth.

Now, let's look at the TRUTH system in greater detail.

T: THE TRIGGER EVENT

This part of the TRUTH system is where reality shows up. Reality may be a minor event, such as someone being a few minutes late for a meeting with you, or it may be a major event, such as the death of a loved one. Regardless of who you are, life will throw all kinds of trigger events at you.

Here are examples of major trigger events. Check any that might apply to you.

_____ Death of a loved one

_____ Divorce

_____ Marital separation

_____ Personal injury or illness

_____ Marriage

_____ Job loss

Here are examples of minor trigger events. Check those that apply to you.

_____ Small weight gain

_____ Interruptions

_____ Home repairs

_____ Too many things to do
_____ Lost or misplaced items
_____ Delays

Before we go on, are there any other trigger events you want to list? Perhaps you'll want to list events that fall between major and minor categories.

_____
_____
_____
_____
_____
_____
_____
_____
_____
_____

U: THE UNHEALTHY RESPONSE

Skipping *R* for a minute, *U* is the part of the TRUTH system where our reaction to the trigger events occurs. Our reaction is usually threefold: physiological, emotional, and behavioral.

Check the physiological reactions that you have experienced during a trigger event.

_____ Fatigue
_____ Dizziness
_____ Sweating
_____ Insomnia
_____ Headaches
_____ Stomach problems

Check the emotional reactions you have felt about a trigger event.

_____ Anxiety

_____ Depression

_____ Anger

_____ Guilt

_____ Resentment

_____ Sadness

Check the behavioral reactions you have experienced following a trigger event.

_____ Withdrawing

_____ Yelling

_____ Shaking

_____ Overworking

_____ Fingernail biting

_____ Overeating

Now take a closer look at your personal health. Complete the following statements pertaining to your physiological condition by identifying the trigger event that prompted the condition. If a statement doesn't apply to you, don't create a problem—just skip over it.

The last time I felt fatigued was

_____

_____

_____.

(For instance, ". . . when I made myself a 'things to do' list and tried to do every item in a short period of time.")

The last time I felt dizzy was

_____

_____

_____.

(For instance, ". . . when I pushed myself too hard at aerobics, trying to lose three pounds in one week.")

I recall breaking out in a nervous sweat

_____

_____

_____.

(For instance, ". . . when I heard a rumor that the company I work for was contemplating a big layoff.")

I last experienced insomnia

_____

_____

_____.

(For instance, ". . . when I paid the bills and realized how bad our money situation was.")

My last headache was

_____

_____

_____.

(For instance, ". . . when my two-year-old made a scene at the grocery store.")

I remember having stomach problems

_____

_____

_____.

(For instance, ". . . after I had an argument with my best friend.")

Do the same for emotional reactions. Complete the following sentences if they apply to your life.

The last time I felt anxious was

_____

_____

_____.

(For instance, ". . . when the morning traffic was much heavier than usual, and I thought I would be late for work.")

I felt depressed

_____

_____

_____.

(For instance, ". . . when I stepped on the bathroom scale and saw that I had gained five pounds.")

I remember feeling angry

_____

_____

_____.

(For instance, ". . . when I was at the store checkout with a sale item, only to find the sale had ended.")

I felt guilty

_____

_____

_____.

(For instance, ". . . the last time I yelled at my spouse.")

I experienced resentment

_____

_____

(For instance, ". . . when someone made a joke at my expense in front of others.")

The last time I felt sad was

_____

_____

(For instance, ". . . when a close friend got fired from his job.")

Finish the personal evaluation by completing these sentences related to behavioral reactions.

I recall withdrawing

_____

_____

(For instance, ". . . when my mother criticized my child rearing methods.")

The last time I yelled was

_____

_____

(For instance, ". . . when my sixteen-year-old broke curfew for the third time in two weeks.")

I remember shaking

_____

_____

(For instance, ". . . when I was under the pressure of a deadline at work.")

I recall creating a work flurry

_____

_____

_____.

(For instance, ". . . after I argued with my spouse, so I worked late at the office to 'hide.'")

The last time I bit my fingernails was

_____

_____

_____.

(For instance, ". . . when I thought I was short of cash and couldn't pay the restaurant bill.")

I overate

_____

_____

_____.

(For instance, ". . . when my kids went off to summer camp for a week.")

THE *T* CAUSES *U* PROBLEM

One of the most destructive mistakes we can make in how we live our lives is believing that trigger events (*T*) *directly* cause our unhealthy reactions (*U*). For example, let's say you are standing in line and someone cuts in front of you (trigger event), and you become extremely angry about it (unhealthy reaction). You might conclude that the person who cut in front of you *caused* your anger, rather than conclude your anger is something you *chose* to feel. As hard as it may be to accept, trigger events do not directly cause our reactions, and we make ourselves victims when we believe they do.

The best practical argument against "*T* causes *U*" thinking is the simple fact that people often experience exactly the same event but react to it in much different ways. Sit in a stadium and watch a football game and you will see what I mean. If the referee makes a questionable call, observe the different reactions between the home fans and the visitors. How could the same event cause two different reactions?

More important, we know that "*T* causes *U*" thinking is a lie because the Bible says so. Recall Proverbs 23:7: "For as he thinks in his heart, so is he." It doesn't say, "As what *happens* to a man, so is he." God holds each of us accountable for how we choose to react to the things that happen to us in life.

Events don't directly cause reactions, no matter how much it may seem that way. Coming to a deeper understanding and acceptance of this truth is essential to emotional and spiritual health.

R: RECKLESS THINKING

This part of the TRUTH system is where you think about the trigger event that just occurred. The way you think about an event will determine your physiological, emotional, and behavioral reaction to it. When you think lies, your reactions to trigger events will be inappropriate and unhealthy. When you think truth, your reaction to trigger events will be appropriate and healthy.

Your thoughts at *R* are the "eyeglasses" through which you perceive the events that show up at *T.* Believing lies is like looking at those events through eyeglasses that distort what you are seeing, causing you to overreact or underreact. Believing truth is like looking at those events through eyeglasses that allow you to see them exactly as they are, helping you to react appropriately.

Let's walk through a scenario to see *T, R,* and *U* in action.

Suppose you are at a very important social event, and you are dressed in an expensive outfit. Suddenly, without warning, a greasy, red-sauced hors d'oeuvre slips off the toothpick you are holding and spills down the front of your shirt or blouse. That is the trigger event that will set everything in motion.

My reaction would be something like this:

Trigger Event: Spilled an hors d'oeuvre on my nice clean shirt.
Reckless Thinking: *Thurman, you stupid idiot. Only a socially ungracious slug like you would do something as stupid as this. No one else at this party did something this stupid. You look like a clown with no circus to go to. Every eye in the place is on you. You will be lucky if you ever get invited to another social event the rest of your life.*
Unhealthy Responses:
Physiological—heart starts to race, muscles tense up, begin to sweat.
Emotional—feel anxious, humiliated, embarrassed, uncomfortable.
Behavioral—immediately cover the spot on my shirt with my hand and hurriedly walk to the rest room where I feverishly work on getting out the stain.

What do you think you would say to yourself if this happened to you? Write down what you think your thoughts would be.

_____

_____

Now apply this to your real-life events. Write down three trigger events that happened to you and your reckless thinking for each trigger event. In other words, what lies did you buy into that caused you to respond the way you did? If you need some help here, go back to chapter 1 and review some of the statements in the self-analysis questionnaire.

1. Trigger Event: _____
Reckless Thinking: _____
_____

2. Trigger Event: _____
Reckless Thinking: _____
_____

3. Trigger Event: _____
Reckless Thinking: _____
_____

Do you see how the reckless thinking contributes to the unhealthy response? Write down a few comments on how the lies you believe affect your responses to each of the trigger events.

My responses to the first scenario: _____
_____
_____

My responses to the second scenario: _____
_____
_____

My responses to the third scenario:_____
_____
_____

T: TRUTHFUL THINKING

The second *T* stands for truthful thinking. Remember, it is at this point that you want to face the real truth about the trigger event. For example, let's go back to spilling the hors d'oeuvre on our nice, clean shirt. We know the trigger event, we dealt with the reckless thinking, and we examined the unhealthy response. What's the truth in this situation? For me, it might be something like this:

Hey, you just made a mistake. It isn't the end of the world. Nobody really noticed, and even if they did, they probably felt some empathy pains for you. Maybe you can even make a joke out of it to put everyone at ease (tell the host or hostess that not only did you enjoy the hors d'oeuvres but your shirt did, too). Be thankful it wasn't battery acid you spilled on your shirt. Now, go clean yourself up and get back to enjoying the party.

Write down what the truth is about spilling something on yourself at an important social event.

_____

_____

_____

_____

How did you do with truthful thinking? How many truths were you able to come up with concerning the event? You may have come up with several, or you may not have come up with any. Perhaps you were somewhere in between. One thing is certain, however: You see that it is a challenge to find and face the truth.

Now, how about your real-life scenarios? What's the truth in each of the situations you identified earlier? Write down your thoughts in the space that's provided. It might be hard at first, but give it a try and stay with it.

The truth about my first scenario:

_____

_____

_____

_____

_____

The truth about my second scenario:

_____

_____

_____

_____

_____

The truth about my third scenario:

_____

_____

_____

_____

_____

H: HEALTHY RESPONSE

After you tell yourself the truth, you can respond to a trigger event in a healthy way. Think back to the stained shirt at the party. Would telling yourself the truth about the situation help calm you down physiologically, emotionally, and behaviorally? Or would you remain upset about the incident?

If the truth would not have calmed you down, ask yourself why. Maybe you have reached a point where the truth doesn't seem true. Maybe your mental truth "muscle" has atrophied through lack of exercise over the years, and the lies you believe are stronger in your mind. Be of good cheer. With practice, the truth can become stronger than anything else in your thoughts, and you can respond to any event in your life in a healthy way.

Describe a healthy response in each of your real-life scenarios.

A healthy response in my first scenario:

_____

_____

_____

_____

_____

A healthy response in my second scenario:

_____

_____

_____

_____

_____

A healthy response in my third scenario:

_____

_____

_____

_____

_____

LOOKING OVER
WHERE WE'VE BEEN

This has been an exciting chapter providing you with a tool that will aid you in your battle for emotional and spiritual health.

In the chapters ahead we will be looking very specifically at the lies we tell ourselves. But since we focused so distinctly on the TRUTH system in this chapter, perhaps the best way to review would be by talking to the God of truth. Take some time to write a prayer to the Lord. In it, thank Him for being the Source of all truth. Then, write to Him about what you learned about yourself in this chapter. He is very interested in you and your struggles in life. Share with Him some of the lies you have believed. Ask for His help in getting back on the path of truth. Speak to God from your heart.

Dear Lord:

_____

_____

_____

_____

_____

_____

_____

_____

_____

_____

_____

_____

_____

GROUP DISCUSSION STARTERS

1. Share with the group a trigger event from your life. Obviously, you want to choose one you are comfortable communicating with others. It may be a funny one or one that's very poignant. You'll be amazed how these sorts of issues can bring a group together.

2. When you worked on the material under the unhealthy response section, did you find you experienced more physiological reactions or emotional reactions or behavioral reactions? Why do you think that is?

3. Coming to grips with the reckless thinking is a big step. What stands out most to you about this aspect of the system?

4. Why is "T causes R causes U" a better way of thinking than "T causes U"?

5. Share with the group the most important truth you learned from this lesson. It may be something very important to the study or it may be a thought that was fleeting. Either way, if it was helpful to you, it is very important.

6. Did this system come easy for you, or do you anticipate it's going to take some practice?

7. How does this system coincide with spiritual maturity? Is this another way to develop the mind of Christ? What spiritual lessons did you learn as a result of this chapter?

8. Get together with your buddy and bring each other up-to-date. Find out how each other's week went, and ask for some specific items to pray about. Continue to be sensitive to your buddy's particular situation. Be a friend.

Chapter 3

DEFEATING SELF LIES

Sally and Janice always looked forward to Wednesday mornings. They had a standing "appointment" with each other for coffee and conversation. They met at each other's house on alternate weeks so their preschool children could accompany them. Sally's three-year-old daughter, Heather, and Janice's two-year-old son, Jason, played together in the family room while their mothers talked at the dining room table.

One Wednesday Sally was particularly looking forward to her conversation with Janice. It had not been a good week from Sally's point of view, and she needed the opportunity to lay it all out for Janice.

"David is not doing well in school," Sally began. "It appears that third grade is more of a challenge to him than any of us realized. His behavior is becoming a problem, and it's really stressing me out!" Sally released a large sigh and stared down at her coffee mug.

As Janice began to ask a question, Sally interrupted, never giving Janice a chance.

"It's not David's fault," Sally continued. "It's that teacher, Miss Drake. She's mean and unreasonable. She's the source of David's problem and my problem."

Janice decided to sit quietly and let Sally get it all out.

"It's not supposed to be this way," Sally whispered, barely holding back the tears. "This was supposed to be such a wonderful year for our family. I really needed things to go smoothly with David so I could feel happy and peaceful again—you know—all that good mother stuff. Anyway, this teacher has upset the applecart with her attitude."

"Have you tried talking with her?" Janice asked.

"Once, just once," replied Sally. "We don't see eye to eye, so it becomes nothing but frustration for me." Sally paused and looked up at Janice sheepishly.

"I have to confess, Miss Drake has tried to call me here at the house several times, but I won't take her calls. I let the answering machine take the message even though I'm right here listening to it. I think it's just easier to avoid her rather than face all this stuff right now."

Janice and Sally tried to continue their conversation, but playtime was over for Heather and Jason. Heather came out of the family room in a huff.

"Jason's not being nice. He doesn't want to play with me. I don't like him. He's a brat. I don't want to play with him anymore."

Lies can enter our lives at a very early age. Look at three-year-old Heather. Things had to go her way for her to be happy. Her unhappiness, she believed, was caused by Jason. So she avoided Jason rather than deal with him. Do you see the parallel between Heather's circumstance and her mother's? Sally used the identical strategy. "Things have to go my way. I'm not happy and it's all Miss Drake's fault. I'd rather avoid Miss Drake than face her."

It was Demosthenes who said,

Nothing is so easy as to deceive one's self; for what we wish we readily believe.

The lies we deceive ourselves with, as Demosthenes suggested, are often what we *wish* were true. When such lies are brought to our attention, we often deny that we believe them because they seem so unrealistic and absurd. Our actions and emotions, however, reveal that we do believe the lies, and these lies greatly influence the way we look at ourselves, others, and the world around us. The lies we will discuss in this chapter are called *self lies,* and through my counseling experiences I have found them to be the most destructive to people. Let's start with one that's rampant in our success-oriented world.

I MUST BE PERFECT

Ron is a great example of a person caught in the perfection trap. He is a superachiever. Ron is convinced he must be *the* best in his business and nothing short of that will do. Ron is driven. Ron is a workaholic. Ron translates satisfaction as achievement.

Ron's need to be perfect was born of a deep sense of worthlessness. He has tried to compensate for feeling worthless by super-accomplishment. Yet nothing he accomplishes makes him feel better about himself.

Perfectionists have unrealistically high standards they have never met and can't possibly meet, yet they hang on to these standards as if they were objects of worship. Even when they feel depressed, they see the idea of changing the standard as blasphemous. In a very painful way, the standards become more important than their very selves.

Do you struggle with the lie, "I must be perfect"? If your answer is yes, you are not alone. Perfectionism has countless people in its grip. Let's look at this issue more closely to see how perfectionism rears its ugly head in your day-to-day world.

Are you a perfectionist at your job? (Circle one.)
Always   *Often*   *Sometimes*   *Never*

If you circled any answer besides *never,* describe a typical example of how you are a perfectionist at your job. *(For instance, "I worked late three nights in a row to finish a report that wasn't due for another month.")*

_____

_____

_____

_____

_____

Are you a perfectionist when it comes to parenting?
(Circle one.)
Always   *Often*   *Sometimes*   *Never*

If you circled any answer besides *never,* describe a typical example of how you are a perfectionist in your parenting. *(For instance, "I won't allow my children to assist me in odd jobs around the house, because they don't do them up to my standards of perfection—so I do them myself.")*

_____

_____

_____

_____

_____

Are you a perfectionist in your relationship with the opposite sex (spouse, boyfriend, girlfriend)? (Circle one.)
Always   *Often*   *Sometimes*   *Never*

If you circled any answer besides *never,* describe a typical example of how you are a perfectionist in your relationship with the opposite sex. *(For instance, "I like my husband to look neat so I am always telling him to fix his collar or tuck in his shirt.")*

_____

_____

_____

_____

_____

Are you a perfectionist while you are at play? (Circle one.)
Always   Often   Sometimes   Never

If you circled any answer besides *never,* describe a typical example of how you are a perfectionist while you play. *(For instance, "I'm having a difficult time finding someone to play golf with me. I am very intense about the game, and my friends feel intimidated around me when I'm on the course.")*

_____

_____

_____

_____

_____

Are there any other comments you want to express concerning your experience with the lie, "I must be perfect"?

_____

_____

_____

_____

_____

A very helpful insight into this lie is in understanding where it came from. Look at the following possibilities.

Did you feel the need to be perfect for your parents when you were a child? _____ How?

_____

_____

_____

_____

_____

Did you feel the need to be perfect in school? _____ How?

_____

_____

_____

_____

_____

Did you feel the need to be perfect in church? _____ How?

_____

_____

_____

_____

_____

Did you feel perfectionism was something society expected? _____ How?

_____

_____

_____

_____

Let's probe a little deeper. Here's a very important distinction I want you to ponder. Look at this question carefully:

What is the difference between *the* best and *your* best?

What is *the* best?

_____

_____

_____

_____

What is *your* best?

_____

_____

_____

_____

What it boils down to is this: We all make mistakes. It's just part of being human. Perfectionism is a hard lie to break. Breaking it demands that the perfectionist treat himself or herself with respect, allowing that mistakes are the rule, not the exception. It means acknowledging that all we can do is our best and learn as we go. It means learning to take satisfaction from a good effort.

Go back over your examples of perfectionism. List some specific ways you can enjoy your best efforts without putting yourself under intense pressure.

Specific things I can do to enjoy my job: *(For instance, "I tend to finish one job and move right to the next one. I'm going to take time to savor each accomplishment.")*

_____

_____

_____
_____
_____

Specific things I can do to enjoy parenting: *(For instance, "I know my seven-year-old really wants to go on a bike ride. I've been putting it off with tons of excuses. No more excuses!")*

_____
_____
_____
_____

Specific things I can do to enjoy my relationship with the opposite sex: *(For instance, "I will become more tolerant of an untucked shirttail. My husband is a wonderful man, and I'd rather have him with his shirttail out than any other man alive!")*

_____
_____
_____
_____

Specific things I can do to enjoy play: *(For instance, "I'm going to play a round of golf just for fun. I may even see how many balls I can put in the lake on purpose!")*

_____
_____
_____
_____

Here is an important truth from the New Testament to offset the lie "I must be perfect":

If we claim to be without sin, we deceive ourselves and the truth is not in us. If we confess our sins, he is faithful and just and will forgive us our sins and purify us from all unrighteousness.

1 John 1:8–9, NIV

Isn't that a great comfort? God knows us, complete with our imperfections, yet He loves us and offers us total forgiveness. Before moving to the next section, take a few minutes to commit these two verses to memory. In doing so, you beat down the lie by holding up the truth.

Last, but not least, take some time to put the TRUTH system to work. As you look back over your struggle with perfectionism, pick a sample trigger event—one that best represents your battle with this lie—and use the following outline to walk through a more healthy response.

Trigger Event: _____

_____

_____

_____

_____

Reckless Thinking: _____

_____

_____

_____

_____

Unhealthy Reaction: _____

_____

_____

_____

_____

Truthful Thinking: _____

_____

_____

_____

_____

Healthy Reaction: _____

_____

_____

_____

I MUST HAVE EVERYONE ELSE'S LOVE AND APPROVAL

Children often learn to believe this lie at an early age. Getting good grades on a report card can be a way for a child to meet approval needs. In this case, getting good grades is less about achieving academic excellence and more about winning Mom and Dad's approval. A child also may seek approval by becoming a "social chameleon," changing her personality and opinions to blend with those of classmates in order to fit in and make everyone "like" her.

The Bible encourages us to serve one another in love and to minister to each other. But we do not obey the Scripture when our motives for serving are to earn love and gain approval.

Is this an area where you struggle? Do you find yourself thinking, *Unless everyone loves me and accepts me, I can't feel good about myself?*

In the spaces that follow, reflect on the people you try to please. You'll be drawn to some more than others, most likely. Give some examples of "pleaser" behaviors.

My parents: *(For instance, "I always made good grades because I wanted my parents to be proud of me.")*

_____

_____

_____

_____

_____

My mate: *(For instance, "I always allow my wife to choose the restaurant we'll eat in because I'm afraid I'll choose a place she won't like.")*

_____

_____

_____

_____

_____

My children: *(For instance, "When my teenager asks for money, I always give him some because I don't want him to think I'm a tightwad.")*

_____

_____

_____

_____

_____

My coworkers: *(For instance, "I know my coworkers are taking advantage of me, but I can't say no to them for fear they won't like me anymore.")*

_____

_____

_____

_____

My friends: *(For instance, "I always baby-sit my friend's three-year-old whenever she asks me, even if there is something else I need to do. I'm afraid she won't be my friend anymore if I say I can't baby-sit.")*

_____

_____

_____

_____

My enemies: *(For instance, "There's a guy at work who is out to get me. He blames his mistakes on me, but I find it very difficult to confront him. He knows this and is using it to his advantage.")*

_____

_____

_____

_____

God: *(For instance, "I know in my heart that God loves me, but my head tells me I have to earn God's love. I am constantly performing to please God.")*

_____

_____

_____

_____

These lies have some pretty serious effects on your thinking. Some of the effects are listed below. Circle whether you agree or disagree with each statement, then explain why.

1. After a period of time, a person loses his/her true identity.

      Agree   *Disagree*

Why? _____

_____

_____

2. The expectations of others are placed above doing what is right.

      Agree   *Disagree*

Why? _____

_____

_____

3. Responsibility is assumed for the other person's interests and perceptions.

      Agree   *Disagree*

Why? _____

_____

_____

4. There is more concern about people thinking well of you than the rightness of the actions taken.

      Agree   *Disagree*

Why? _____

_____

_____

5. Emotional well-being is put into someone else's hands, who may not have your best interests at heart.

      Agree   *Disagree*

Why? _____

_____

_____

When a person believes this lie, the person creates tension in his or her relationship with God. Put simply, trying to please people often stands in the way of pleasing God. Look at the apostle Paul's words to the believers in Galatia:

> Am I now trying to win the approval of men, or of God? Or am I trying to please men? If I were still trying to please men, I would not be a servant of Christ.
>
> Galatians 1:10, NIV

Take a moment to meditate on that truth. If this is an area of concern for you, memorize this verse. Ask God to place it in the front of your thinking so it will have its rightful effect on your life.

Go back over your notes in this section and pick the best example of your belief in this lie. Now put it to the TRUTH system.

Trigger Event: _____

_____

_____

_____

_____

Reckless Thinking: _____

_____

_____

_____

_____

Unhealthy Reaction: _____

_____

_____

_____

_____

Truthful Thinking: _____

_____

_____

_____

_____

Healthy Reaction: _____

_____

_____

_____

_____

IT IS EASIER TO AVOID PROBLEMS THAN TO FACE THEM

A friend of mine loves to tell the story of playing hide-and-seek with his son, when his son was a toddler. When it was Daddy's turn to hide, my friend would dutifully hunt out a hiding spot in the apartment that would be easy for a two-year-old to discover without too much effort.

The real fun, however, was when it was his son's turn to hide. As Dad counted to one hundred, his boy would run to the other side of the room and simply put his two little hands over his eyes. Obviously the boy wasn't hidden, so it made for quite an acting job for Dad not to find him too soon!

Do you see the little boy's logic? In his two-year-old mind he thought, _I can't see you, so you must not be able to see me!_

Avoiding problems is part of our human nature, but some of us carry it to an unhealthy extreme. We have believed a lie that says our problems will go away if we avoid them. The truth is, we're asking for more serious problems when we run from problems. In his fine book *The Road Less Traveled*, M. Scott Peck writes:

> Fearing the pain involved, almost all of us, to a greater or lesser degree, attempt to avoid problems. We procrastinate, hoping that they will go away. We ignore them, forget them, pretend they do not exist. . . . We attempt to get out of them rather than suffer through them.
>
> This tendency to avoid problems and the emotional suffering inherent in them is the primary basis of all human mental illness.

Did you catch that? People who avoid their pain usually end up with more pain in the long run. People who face their pain save themselves a great deal of unnecessary suffering down the road. It's as simple as that.

The following is a list of common avoidance behaviors. Circle the answers that best describe your particular situation. Be honest. Don't create a problem, but don't avoid one, either!

1. I wait until the last possible moment to do an unpleasant task.

   Always   *Often*   *Sometimes*   *Never*

2. I put off making an appointment with the dentist.

   Always   *Often*   *Sometimes*   *Never*

3. If there's a problem, I talk to someone not directly concerned.

   Always   *Often*   *Sometimes*   *Never*

4. When arguing, I talk about "sideline" issues, not the real ones.

Always   Often   Sometimes   Never

5. I save the hardest work until last.

Always   Often   Sometimes   Never

How did you do? Is this a problem in your life? Let me raise another aspect of this problem. I am particularly concerned that too many parents today are unnecessarily rescuing their children from problems in misguided love powered by this lie. When parents make a habit of rescuing their child, the child begins believing this lie, too, and it soon becomes engrained as "truth." The parents haven't done the child a favor. They've deprived the child of chances to develop appropriate coping skills he'll need when life, and all its unavoidable pain, hits him head-on in adulthood. I firmly believe, barring certain situations beyond the child's ability to cope, that children need to be responsible for facing their own problems.

If you are a parent, how do you measure up in this realm of rescuing? Use the exercise below to reflect on your rescuing relationship with each of your children. In the first blank fill in the child's name, then give examples of how you have rescued the child.

Do I tend to rescue _____? In what ways? *(For instance, "I'll stay up late doing his homework because he didn't complete his assignment.")*

_____

_____

_____

Do I tend to rescue _____? In what ways?

_____

_____

_____

Do I tend to rescue _____? In what ways?

_____

_____

_____

Do I tend to rescue _____? In what ways?

_____

_____

_____

Let's confront this issue head-on. Read the following eight statements. Circle whether you agree or disagree with each statement, and then write down your reasoning.

1. Problems don't just go away. They pile up day after day.

      Agree   *Disagree*

Why? _____

_____

_____

2. Avoidance is not an escape, it is a postponement.

      Agree   *Disagree*

Why? _____

_____

_____

3. Suffering must be endured until the problem is faced.

      Agree   *Disagree*

Why? _____

_____

_____

4. Problems often grow in magnitude if they are left unat-
tended.

        Agree   *Disagree*

Why? _____

_____

_____

5. When a problem is faced, it is seldom as bad as it was
imagined to be.

        Agree   *Disagree*

Why? _____

_____

_____

6. People who avoid pain usually end up with more pain in
the long run.

        Agree   *Disagree*

Why? _____

_____

_____

7. Our greatest successes come from facing problems.

        Agree   *Disagree*

Why? _____

_____

_____

8. Avoided problems come back again.

        Agree   *Disagree*

Why? _____

_____

_____

The Bible is very clear on the role of suffering in our lives. It'll be there. Count on it. Expect it. Nobody is exempt from problems. God wants us to see the positive effects problems can bring to our lives. Think about these verses from the book of Philippians:

> I want to know Christ and the power of his resurrection and the fellowship of sharing in his sufferings, becoming like him in his death, and so, somehow, to attain to the resurrection from the dead.
>
> Not that I have already obtained all this, or have already been made perfect, but I press on to take hold of that for which Christ Jesus took hold of me. Philippians 3:10–12, NIV

Do you believe the lie, "It is easier to avoid problems than to face them"? If so, take the best representative example from your life and put it through the TRUTH system.

Trigger Event: _____

_____

_____

_____

_____

Reckless Thinking: _____

_____

_____

_____

Unhealthy Reaction: _____

_____

_____

_____

_____

Truthful Thinking: _____

_____

_____

_____

_____

Healthy Reaction: _____

_____

_____

_____

_____

I CAN'T BE HAPPY UNLESS THINGS GO MY WAY

Barry is a control freak. You know the type. It's his way or no way at all. He precisely plans his schedules and routines. Now don't get me wrong, there's something quite admirable about a person who is dependable and punctual and reliable. But, like the other lies we have examined, good things can be taken to unhealthy extremes. Barry can't enjoy life unless it goes according to his script. At work, he gets anxious when his appointments run late. At lunch, he can't enjoy his meal if the service is too slow. And traffic—WOW! Don't get Barry in a traffic jam or a rush hour bumper-to-bumper situation. He just doesn't cope well.

I often refer to this lie as the "My Way" lie. Those of us who suffer from the My Way lie tend to believe the world should revolve around us. This narcissistic style of living makes us miserable. It makes placing ourselves in another person's shoes impossible, and that incapacity makes healthy and stable relationships impossible.

There is a wonderful illustration in the Old Testament of a man who thought his way was the right way and that is what he wanted. The man's name is Jonah. Look at this brief account:

> Jonah went out and sat down at a place east of the city. There he made himself a shelter, sat in its shade and waited to see what would happen to the city. Then the LORD God provided a vine and made it grow up over Jonah to give shade for his head to ease his discomfort, and Jonah was very happy about the vine. But at dawn the next day God provided a worm, which chewed the vine so that it withered. When the sun rose, God provided a scorching east wind, and the sun blazed on Jonah's head so that he grew faint. He wanted to die, and said, "It would be better for me to die than to live."
>
> But God said to Jonah, "Do you have a right to be angry about the vine?"
>
> "I do," he said. "I am angry enough to die."
>
> But the LORD said, "You have been concerned about this vine, though you did not tend it or make it grow. It sprang up overnight and died overnight. But Nineveh has more than a hundred and twenty thousand people who cannot tell their right hand from their left, and many cattle as well. Should I not be concerned about that great city?"
>
> Jonah 4:5–11, NIV

God wanted Jonah to go to Nineveh, but Jonah was a firm believer in My Way. Read the following statements and circle whether you believe the statement is true or false.

1. As far as Jonah was concerned, Jonah's way was the right way.

       True   *False*

2. Jonah's concern was for his own satisfaction, not for what God wanted.

        True   *False*

3. Jonah believed in his right to have what he wanted.

        True   *False*

4. Jonah's personal satisfaction was in conflict with God's plan.

        True   *False*

Use Jonah's illustration as a springboard to personal examination. Do you believe the lie, "I can't be happy unless things go my way"?

Do you place requirements on having a good day? List them: *(For instance, "I must not be late for work, the sun must be shining, I must eat a hot breakfast," etc.)*

   1. _____
   2. _____
   3. _____
   4. _____
   5. _____
   6. _____

Now go back over your list and write down how each of those issues is not totally under your control.

   1. _____
   2. _____
   3. _____
   4. _____
   5. _____
   6. _____

So what can you do to make each day a good day? Read the following statements and under each one, record your reaction to it. Specifically ask yourself, "How can I apply this statement to *my* life?"

1. Understand that God is in control, working His plan, which is best.

    My response: _____
    _____
    _____
    _____

2. Stop expecting others to satisfy all my needs.

    My response: _____
    _____
    _____
    _____

3. Be as concerned for the welfare of others as I am for myself.

    My response: _____
    _____
    _____
    _____

4. Allow other people the freedom to make wrong decisions.

    My response: _____
    _____
    _____
    _____

5. Learn to be flexible, to cope with whatever life throws my way.

My response: _____

_____

_____

_____

6. Learn to be content in spite of what gets in my way; God's grace is sufficient.

My response: _____

_____

_____

_____

Once again, look at a verse from the apostle Paul's writings to the church at Philippi:

> I am not saying this because I am in need, for I have learned to be content whatever the circumstances. I know what it is to be in need, and I know what it is to have plenty. I have learned the secret of being content in any and every situation, whether well fed or hungry, whether living in plenty or in want. I can do everything through him who gives me strength.
>
> Philippians 4:11–13, NIV

Now there's a truth that's truly liberating. Do you know the secret of being content that Paul referred to in these verses? Take these verses and make them your own. Take a few minutes right now and offer these words of Paul as your personal prayer to God. Talk to Him openly.

The TRUTH system will work against the lie, "I can't be happy unless things go my way." Pick your best example of believing this lie and apply it below.

Trigger Event: _____

_____

_____
_____
_____
_____

Reckless Thinking: _____
_____
_____
_____
_____

Unhealthy Reaction: _____
_____
_____
_____

Truthful Thinking: _____
_____
_____
_____

Healthy Reaction: _____
_____
_____
_____

IT'S SOMEBODY ELSE'S FAULT

This lie allows me to pass the buck for all my emotional upsets onto anybody or anything nearby. It points a finger outward. No responsibility is taken here.

_____

Do any of the following statements ring true in your life? If so, jot down an example of when it occurred.

1. "You make me mad when you do that!"
A personal example: *(For instance, "I missed the green light at a busy intersection because the person in the car in front of me was driving too slowly.")*

_____

_____

_____

_____

_____

2. "The reason I can't get anything done is that people are constantly interrupting me!"
A personal example: *(For instance, "I was trying to do some yard work last Saturday, but my ten-year-old kept interrupting me.")*

_____

_____

_____

_____

_____

3. "I don't enjoy my job because all the people I work with irritate me!"
A personal example: *(For instance, "Frank thinks he's a stand-up comedian at the plant. His jokes are not funny, and he distracts me and the other workers.")*

_____

_____

_____

_____

_____

4. "I don't go to church anymore because the people there are not friendly and they make me feel uncomfortable."

A personal example: *(For instance, "I felt uncomfortable when people at church kept asking me about my teenage son who wasn't attending with me at the time. I felt judged, condemned, guilty.")*

_____

_____

_____

_____

_____

This lie really speaks to one of the central issues of this entire workbook: *Events do not cause emotional reactions. We cannot blame other people or events for our feelings because our feelings are caused by our thoughts. Since no one forces us to think the way we think, we are responsible for the feelings our thoughts create. Our unhappiness or happiness is our "fault."*

Blaming someone else is as old as humankind. It first occurred in the Garden of Eden between Adam, Eve, and God:

And he said, "Who told you that you were naked? Have you eaten from the tree that I commanded you not to eat from?"

The man said, "The woman you put here with me—she gave me some fruit from the tree, and I ate it."

Then the LORD God said to the woman, "What is this you have done?"

The woman said, "The serpent deceived me, and I ate."

Genesis 3:11–13, NIV

Adam and Eve *chose* to sin, but they found someone to blame for their choices. It has been that way ever since, hasn't it?

Why would a person want to blame someone else?

_____

_____

_____

_____

_____

Apply the TRUTH system to the lie, "It's somebody else's fault." Review your personal examples of buying into this lie, select the best representative, and walk it through the system.

Trigger Event: _____

_____

_____

_____

Reckless Thinking: _____

_____

_____

_____

Unhealthy Reaction: _____

_____

_____

_____

Truthful Thinking: _____

_____

_____

_____

_____

Healthy Reaction: _____

_____

_____

_____

_____

LOOKING OVER
WHERE WE'VE BEEN

Of the five self lies we covered, there may be one that is particularly troubling to you. Rather than review all five, go back to that one specific lie and look over your notes. Use the space below to write yourself a letter. Make it a letter of truth. Retell yourself the truths you have learned to offset the lie that nags you. Talk about what you will do differently as a result of this lesson. Set yourself some realistic goals. Rehearse what God has taught you about yourself.

Dear _____,

_____

_____

_____

_____

_____

_____

_____

_____

_____

_____

_____

_____

Signed, _____

GROUP DISCUSSION STARTERS

1. Ask someone in the group to recount a humorous situation where a trigger event exposed a self lie to the person. Maybe the trigger event was leaving a child at church, locking the keys in the car, or being stuck in traffic!

2. The lie of perfection is a biggie. How do you differentiate between perfectionism and trying to be the best you can be? (This issue could use up your entire time for discussion!)

3. What is the relationship between receiving everyone's love/approval and your self-esteem?

4. Respond to Scott Peck's quote, "This tendency to avoid problems and the emotional suffering inherent in them is the primary basis of all human mental illness."

5. Have someone in the group read aloud Philippians 4:11–13. What does it mean to you to "be content whatever the circumstances"? How does this issue apply directly to your spiritual life? Use the most practical terms possible.

6. When we believe the lie, "It's somebody else's fault," we seek to blame another person for our situation. Why do people want to blame someone else?

7. How can a person defeat a lie? Discuss the TRUTH system within your group. Spend some time with your buddy, checking in on his or her needs and prayer requests. Find a practical way to encourage your buddy this week.

Chapter 4

DEFEATING WORLDLY LIES

Wouldn't it be amazing if all advertisements were true? We'd all love to be admired by others because we drive the best car, cure damaged hair with the right shampoo, and jump like an NBA superstar because we drink a particular soft drink. But, alas, not all advertisements are true. In a childlike way, we want to believe them, but if we do we're headed for disappointment.

Most of us seldom test the validity of the messages swirling around us. And the more we listen and believe, the more needless emotional misery we create for ourselves. In this chapter, we will examine the most widespread and dangerous of these worldly lies.

YOU CAN HAVE IT ALL

Ted and Veronica had been married for sixteen years when the marriage started to unravel. Veronica had chosen to stay at home to be a full-time mother to their three children. She began to feel less and less fulfilled, sensing there was more "out there" in life. She began to spend more and more time away from home. "I feel smothered here at the house," she announced to Ted. "So, I want a divorce. I just know that I can find what I've been missing in my life. I've done the wife thing, I've done the mom thing. Now I want the rest of life. I want to have it all."

Like many people, Veronica is moving from one lifestyle to another in a vain attempt to "have it all." The saddest part of the story is most folks don't find what they're looking for. It's a myth, a lie. You can't have it all.

Do you struggle with this in your life? Do you entertain secret thoughts of "having it all"? Linked with this desire is "the grass is always greener on the other side of the fence" type thinking. We may become envious of another person's situation. For instance, a woman who works in the home may envy a woman who works outside the home, and vice versa. A person who works in a large corporation may envy a person who is self-employed, and vice versa. Some single people envy the companionship of married couples, and some married people envy the freedom of single people. The list can go on and on.

Take a minute to identify areas where envy exists in your life.

I envy _____

_____

I envy _____

_____

I envy _____

_____

Where do you think you learned that kind of thinking? *(For instance, from parents, advertisements, teachers, siblings, friends.)*

_____

_____

_____

We need to consider the built-in problems that go along with the lie, "You can have it all." The pursuit of having it all leads to some tough issues.

What problems result from trying to have it all? Look at the following list of statements, then circle whether you agree or disagree with each statement.

1. There is guaranteed failure.

       Agree   *Disagree*

2. The greater the gain, the greater the desire to gain more becomes.

       Agree   *Disagree*

3. Gratitude for God's blessing is replaced by a lack of appreciation.

       Agree   *Disagree*

4. Happiness becomes dependent upon things and obtaining more of them.

       Agree   *Disagree*

I have *never* met a person who really had it all. Never! Think of that someone who you think has it all. Odds are, if you scratched the surface of that someone's life, you'd find a life with painful gaps.

The best case study for this lie is found in the Old Testament. According to the biblical record, King Solomon was the wealthiest and wisest man on earth during his lifetime. Did he think he had it all? Listen to his words:

> Yet when I surveyed all that my hands had done
>> and what I had toiled to achieve,
> everything was meaningless, a chasing after the wind;
>> nothing was gained under the sun.
>>> Ecclesiastes 2:11, NIV

So, if you can't have it all, what should you believe? How do you replace this lie with the truth? The truth can be summarized in one key statement: *contentment* is found in God, not things. Check out these Scriptures:

> But if we have food and clothing, we will be content with that.
>> 1 Timothy 6:8, NIV

> Be content with what you have, because God has said,
>> "Never will I leave you;
>> never will I forsake you."
>>> Hebrews 13:5, NIV

Take a few minutes to let that truth sink in. "Having it all" is a lie, an impossible, unhealthy dream that cheapens the rest of life, making us live for the future instead of enjoying the present. Very few of us are immune to it, but all of us have the choice whether to live by it.

If having it all is an issue for you, walk through the TRUTH system with a sample trigger event that best illustrates your struggle. Carry it through to its conclusion of a healthy response based on truth.

Trigger Event: _____

_____

_____

_____

_____

Reckless Thinking: _____

_____

_____

_____

_____

Unhealthy Reaction: _____

_____

_____

_____

_____

Truthful Thinking: _____

_____

_____

_____

_____

Healthy Reaction: _____

_____

_____

_____

_____

YOU ARE ONLY AS GOOD AS WHAT YOU DO

Travis was a self-made man. He was proud of several ways he was different from his friends. By his best estimation, he was the richest guy in his group. And it was important to couple that with the fact that he was the youngest in his group, as well. Travis valued his drive. He was successful because he wasn't the kind of guy to wait for something to come his way—he went out and got it.

But lately Travis has been hounded by a nagging thought that he needs to do more. He had many successes in his past, but no significant accomplishments recently. After all, you're only as good as what you do, right?

Travis is an example of a person who believes this lie. It's not just a condition of the successful. It can affect anyone, no matter what his socioeconomic level.

Do you feel pressured to perform? Can you see how this pressure is epidemic in our American culture? Think back to your childhood. Did you feel pressure to perform then? Jot down examples as they come to mind. Use the following examples to jog your memory.

Pressure to perform in school:

_____

_____

_____

Pressure to perform in sports:

_____

_____

_____

Pressure to perform in extracurricular activities:

_____

_____

_____

Pressure to perform at church:

_____

_____

_____

Pressure to perform around my friends:

_____

_____

_____

Pressure to perform in my early jobs:

_____

_____

_____

Pressure to perform around my brothers and sisters:

_____

_____

_____

Pressure to perform around my parents:

_____

_____

_____

Now, let's turn the tables. If you are a parent with children at home, are you instilling this lie in your children? Are you passing on conditional or unconditional love?

How do you balance "doing your best" with "unconditional acceptance"?

_____

_____

_____

We live in a world that tells us in no uncertain terms that our self-worth is based on what we do and not the God who made us. This is a destructive lie. We must ask ourselves, What should be the basis for self-worth? I believe that comes solely from God. We need to view ourselves in a "vertical" dimension, seeing who we are in God's eyes, not in a "horizontal" dimension, seeing ourselves through the eyes of others.

The world is obsessed with externals. Jesus denounced this idea in the gospel of Matthew:

> "Woe to you, teachers of the law and Pharisees, you hypocrites! You are like whitewashed tombs, which look beautiful on the outside but on the inside are full of dead men's bones and everything unclean."
>
> Matthew 23:27, NIV

God wants us to understand how unique we really are. Look at the familiar words of the psalmist:

> I praise you because I am fearfully and wonderfully made;
>> your works are wonderful,
> I know that full well.
>
> Psalm 139:14, NIV

God created us in His image. Now that is a true basis for personal worth. Living this truth, though, is harder than believing it. How can we find an appropriate sense of worth in a world that focuses on what we do instead of who made us? Yet overcoming this lie and the exhausting effort that it commands is all that keeps us from going down the same sad road of futility that King Solomon did.

Who am I without what I do? Essentially, we all have to ask ourselves this question if we're ever going to find a solid basis for understanding our worth. Then we have to work at giving ourselves a solid answer.

"You are only as good as what you do" is a lie. If you struggle with this error, pinpoint a trigger event and go through the TRUTH system.

Trigger Event: _____
_____
_____
_____
_____

Reckless Thinking: _____
_____
_____
_____
_____

Unhealthy Reaction: _____
_____
_____
_____
_____

Truthful Thinking: _____
_____
_____
_____
_____

Healthy Reaction: _____
_____
_____
_____
_____

LIFE SHOULD BE EASY

All of us, to a certain degree, attempt to minimize pain and maximize pleasure. Yet this tendency is often at odds with reality, the truth about life as it really is. Life is not easy. It is painful in ways that we need to accept rather than fight.

Jenny struggles with the lie that life should be easy. She is a woman in her thirties who has begun to feel pain in different areas of her life. She feels people dump on her at work, thus concluding that everyone else's job is fine but hers is lousy. She looks at other parents with their kids and concludes that the other children are "angels" and her two kids are "brats." Even her husband doesn't measure up. "Why can't he be more attentive to making my life more enjoyable?" she laments.

Does this type of thinking strike a chord in your life? Have you experienced your share of hardships? Did you also discover that in the midst of this pain there was a valuable lesson to be learned? Can you recall some of these situations? Use the chart below as a reminder.

My experience with physical pain: *(For instance, "I was in an auto accident and needed twelve stitches on my forehead.")*

_____

_____

My lesson from physical pain: *(For instance, "I had to reassess the whole issue of physical beauty. I began to use more 'vertical' thinking—seeing myself as God sees me.")*

_____

_____

_____

My experience with relational pain: *(For instance, "I had to deal with my mate's infidelities.")*

_____

_____

_____

My lesson from relational pain: *(For instance, "I learned I must develop my security and identity in Christ and not base both in being a spouse.")*

_____

_____

_____

My experience with emotional pain: *(For instance, "I went through a horrible period of depression for about two months.")*

_____

_____

_____

My lesson from emotional pain: *(For instance, "I learned that I can choose how I want to feel. It really is up to me.")*

_____

_____

_____

My experience with spiritual pain: *(For instance, "I prayed regularly for a particular request, but God never allowed it to occur.")*

_____

_____

_____

My lesson from spiritual pain: *(For instance, "I learned that God doesn't always answer 'Yes.' Sometimes it's 'No.' Yet God still wants the best for me.")*

_____

_____

_____

_____

Circle whether you agree or disagree with the following statements.

1. We tend to want to hear about comfort, but not about pain.

       Agree   *Disagree*

2. A great deal of hardship and frustration is built into life.

       Agree   *Disagree*

3. True Christian living demands tremendous sacrifice that hurts.

       Agree   *Disagree*

4. The willingness to face problems is paramount to a healthy life.

       Agree   *Disagree*

5. Life is not easy, no matter who you are.

       Agree   *Disagree*

Jesus instructed His disciples concerning this issue. Right before He was arrested and crucified, He told them:

"I have told you these things, so that in me you may have peace. In this world you will have trouble. But take heart! I have overcome the world."

                                John 16:33, NIV

Take a few minutes to memorize that verse. It contains vital truth for all Christians.

I think one of the best promises that Christianity offers is "all things work together for good to those who love God, to those who are the called according to His purpose" (Rom. 8:28). And it's something we need to understand while coping with the "easy life" lie. God doesn't promise there won't be any misfortune or trouble in our lives. He does promise good can come out of bad, but only with effort on our part to realize the final good.

Is there a trigger event that prompts this process in your mind? If so, jot it down below and proceed to follow through the TRUTH system.

Trigger Event: _____
_____
_____
_____

Reckless Thinking: _____
_____
_____
_____

Unhealthy Reaction: _____
_____
_____
_____

Truthful Thinking: _____
_____
_____
_____

Healthy Reaction: _____

_____

_____

_____

LIFE SHOULD BE FAIR

Brandon and Dory always got home from school before Mom and Dad returned from their respective jobs. As the older of the two, Brandon was in charge of the after-school snack. It was usually something as simple as two apples, but every once in a while, Mom would have a batch of brownies waiting for her two little cherubs. Brandon would cut two pieces, give one to Dory, and keep the other for himself. Brandon claimed to always cut the two pieces "exactly alike," yet his sister always complained. Truth be told, the size of the two pieces weren't even close. Brandon was taking advantage of his sister's naiveté and the fact that no adults were around to catch him!

Dory began to complain to her mom upon her arrival from work. "It's not fair!" groaned Dory. "His piece is huge and mine is wimpy!"

"Nope. They're exactly alike," boasted Brandon, relishing his position of power.

"Somebody's not telling the truth," Mom concluded. But neither child would budge from his or her respective position.

Mom solved the dilemma by using the wisdom that God reserves especially for mothers. "Okay, from now on this is how we'll do it," she began. "Brandon, you may continue to cut two pieces 'exactly alike,' but you must show Dory both pieces, and she gets to choose which one she wants. Now that's fair."

Needless to say, Brandon began cutting two brownies that were equal in size.

Whenever our mom said, "That's fair," it struck a pleasing

chord within us. We heard what we wanted to hear. All of us want life to be fair. It speaks of character and caring that Mom worked it all out for us. Unfortunately, we ended up thinking that life would always be that way, which it most definitely is not.

Has life been unfair to you? If you can't answer "Yes," you are a rather unusual individual. We've all been dealt some unfair blows in life. Can you recall a few? Use the list below as an aid.

Unfairness at my job: *(For instance, "My superior messed up a meeting, but I got blamed.")*

_____

_____

_____

Unfairness at home: *(For instance, "I clean up all the time and nobody helps me.")*

_____

_____

_____

Unfairness in the lives of my children: *(For instance, "I had to watch as my son was overlooked for the lead in the school play because the director chose the 'teacher's pet' for the part.")*

_____

_____

_____

Unfairness in my personal life: *(For instance, "I militantly watch my diet. I only eat healthy foods. At my latest physical exam, the doctor told me I have some serious heart and blood pressure problems that need to be monitored. All I can think of is my best friend, who eats like a pig and doesn't have any of these problems.")*

_____

_____

_____

Now that you've thought about some of the unfair situations from the past, I must stress an important principle: *Forgive it!* It's up to us to handle unfairness so we don't pay for it twice—once when it happened, and again when we allow it to wreck our present lives. It's not in the past if you keep reliving it. By separating the past from the present and forgiving those who have treated you unfairly, you can step out of the victim's role and cope with current realities better.

Life isn't fair. That's the truth. Take a trigger event that sparks your thinking, and use the TRUTH system to produce a healthy reaction to this issue.

Trigger Event: _____

_____

_____

Reckless Thinking: _____

_____

_____

_____

Unhealthy Reaction: _____

_____

_____

_____

Truthful Thinking: _____

_____

_____

_____

Healthy Reaction: _____

_____

_____

_____

DON'T WAIT

"Do not store up for yourselves treasures on earth, where moth
and rust destroy, and where thieves break in and steal. But store
up for yourselves treasures in heaven, where moth and rust do
not destroy, and where thieves do not break in and steal."

Matthew 6:19–20, NIV

I don't think this teaching would win Jesus any popularity
contests in today's world. These verses sound like delayed gratification to me. And everyone knows that just won't cut it in our
modern culture. This is an offshoot of the "You Can Have It All"
lie. Since you can have it all, why wait?

Nothing plays up this lie as effectively as the credit card. It
seems American finance is built on the realization that most
Americans will spend way beyond their means if given the opportunity. Many of us will read that verse from Matthew and conclude, "Well, at least I'm not storing up treasure on earth—I'm
spending it as fast as I earn it!"

Let's ease into this issue on a personal level.

Do you know someone who typifies this "instant gratification"
lie? Who?

_____

_____

How do you deal with instant gratification? If *10* is *great* and *1* is *lousy,* where do you rate yourself?

(Circle one.)   1   2   3   4   5   6   7   8   9   10

Why? _____

_____

Is there any pattern to your instant gratification? For example, do the items you can't resist purchasing fall into a category, such as clothing, power tools, books?

_____

_____

This is an important question, so think about it carefully. Is it possible that instant gratification is tied to a deeper need, such as the need for love, comfort, and attention? In other words, do you seek immediate pleasure when what you really need is intimacy? State your reaction to these questions.

_____

_____

_____

_____

Of all people, Christians should understand the concept of waiting. The importance of waiting on God is stamped on almost every page of the Bible. King David wrote it this way:

> Wait on the LORD;
> Be of good courage,
> And He shall strengthen your heart.
>
> Psalm 27:14

This is a great verse, isn't it? Take a few minutes to personalize these three lines in your own words.

_____

_____

_____

_____

This is the truth we need to tell ourselves. The world feeds us the lie that we'll be better off if we whip out the credit card or shortcut the degree or don't hold back on the impulse to tell off a person who has offended us. If the "Don't Wait" lie hits you close to home, take some time before moving on to work through a trigger event with the TRUTH system.

Trigger Event: _____

_____

_____

_____

Reckless Thinking: _____

_____

_____

_____

Unhealthy Reaction: _____

_____

_____

_____

Truthful Thinking: _____

_____

_____

_____

Healthy Reaction: _____

_____

_____

_____

PEOPLE ARE BASICALLY GOOD

"He seemed like such a nice guy."

That's all the Jensens could say about the man who came into their small grocery one day. He produced a business card and introduced himself as a district representative of a large grocery chain. As he made his presentation, he told the Jensens how they could move out of their small mom-and-pop grocery to a large store in an enviable location and enjoy the power and status of a national name. The only question was if they could come up with the $100,000 necessary for start-up costs. "But that should be easy," he said. "Just sell this store and reinvest your profits."

And that's exactly what the Jensens did. They sold their store and gave the $100,000 to this "nice man." Unfortunately, the man was a criminal. He did not work for the grocery chain he claimed to. He took the Jensens' money—their life savings—and skipped town. He was never found.

I truly hope that you have never experienced a lesson with such severe financial ramifications, but perhaps you have been a victim of the lie, "People are basically good."

Have you ever been "burned" because you trusted someone? If so, explain:

_____

_____

_____

_____

_____

Does it sound strange for a psychologist to suggest that believing people are good by nature is a lie?

The idea that our nature is flawed tends to threaten us because it forces us to give up cherished notions about our own goodness. But I think I can point to three sources of evidence that the scales of human nature tip toward bad rather than good.

First, on an interpersonal level (people interacting with people), the history of humankind is marked by greed, hatred, conflict, and murder more than selflessness, love, and peace. The holocaust and the threat of nuclear war in this century are enough to prove my point.

Second, on an intrapersonal level (occurring within ourselves), individuals seem bent toward self-destruction as much as self-growth. Physically, many people do not exercise enough or eat a balanced diet. Emotionally, many people are plagued by some degree of turmoil, often severe enough to require professional help. Mentally, people often have faulty ways of viewing themselves, others, and life in general. Spiritually, many people do not seek God or any form of meaning in life with much consistency or depth. In fact, many people feel that life doesn't really have much purpose to it at all.

Third, I believe the Bible teaches that we are corrupted by a sinful nature, which will ultimately destroy us if we do not allow God to bring it under control.

> The acts of the sinful *nature* are obvious: sexual immorality, impurity and debauchery . . . hatred, discord, jealousy . . . selfish ambition, dissensions, factions and envy; drunkenness, orgies, and the like.
>
> Galatians 5:19–21, NIV (emphasis added)

Not exactly a great picture of what our basic nature is like when it is not yielded to God, is it? I want to make it clear, though, that I don't agree with people who say we are worthless slime. We are created in God's image, and God doesn't make junk. Like it or not, though, we are bent toward evil. Without God's help, we will stay that way.

Do you agree or disagree with the following statements? Circle the appropriate response.

1. If you believe people are basically good, relationships inevitably turn sour when expectations are not met.

Agree   *Disagree*

2. If you believe people are basically good, you will wind up feeling used and hurt.

Agree   *Disagree*

3. If you believe people are basically good, you expect the people around you to be virtuous; healthy realism would serve you better.

Agree   *Disagree*

4. In balancing this issue, we need not conclude that all people are scum and can never be trusted.

Agree   *Disagree*

5. We need to recognize a person's potential for good and encourage his or her growth without assuming ahead of time how they will act.

Agree   *Disagree*

6. Hold off any assumptions about people. Wait and see what they do.

Agree   *Disagree*

We need a moderate approach to ourselves and others. What I see as the truth in this issue can be summed up in one statement:

People are bent toward sinning, capable of doing good, and in need of God's help to avoid being ruled by evil.

That's the truth. When have you believed the lie, "People are basically good"? Take an example through the TRUTH system.

Trigger Event: _____

_____

_____

_____

Reckless Thinking: _____

_____

_____

_____

Unhealthy Reaction: _____

_____

_____

_____

Truthful Thinking: _____

_____

_____

_____

Healthy Reaction: _____

_____

_____

_____

LOOKING OVER
WHERE WE'VE BEEN

Which worldly lie do you find most damaging in your life?

Check one:
☐ You can have it all.
☐ You are only as good as what you do.
☐ Life should be easy.
☐ Life should be fair.
☐ Don't wait.
☐ People are basically good.

You don't have to deal with this lie alone. Who can you discuss this issue with?

_____

_____

What have you learned about yourself in general through your interaction with the material in this chapter? *(For instance, "I have suffered some damage in my life because I thought I am only as worthwhile as what I do. I'm obsessed with performance and I really need to work on this.")*

_____

_____

_____

_____

One thing I've done that I can feel good about is

_____

_____

_____

I need to follow up on

_____

_____

_____.

An important new insight I've gained is

_____

_____

_____.

GROUP DISCUSSION STARTERS

1. How have you been led to believe that "You can have it all"? Share with the group how the culture affected you by its teachings, its advertisements, its subtle messages, and its not-so-subtle messages. Is it more difficult on your kids in today's world?

2. How does a person go about creating an accurate sense of worth? How do you balance "who you are" with "what you do"? How are you teaching this important issue to your children?

3. "Life should be easy" is a lie. Think back to one of the hardest days of your life. Can you remember it well enough to share it with the group? Did you think you were alone in life's difficulty? What got you through that trying time?

4. How do you reconcile the theological fact that God is a God of love and justice, yet life is not always fair? Are there any Bible verses that help ease this seeming tension? How would you explain this issue to a new Christian?

5. What have you observed concerning the "Don't Wait" lie and the financial picture in our country? The sexual situation in

our country? Why is delayed gratification so difficult for Americans? What role does the media play in this lie?

6. Do you think people are inherently bad or good? What has been the result of this thinking in your personal experience? Do you think it's necessary to strike a balance here?

7. Spend some time with your buddy. Which worldly lie creates the biggest struggle for him/her? Is there a tangible way in which you can be of assistance? What sorts of prayer requests can you remember for this session? Go back over some of the other issues you two have been working on, and give each other an update.

Chapter 5

DEFEATING MARITAL LIES

When Sam and Laura came for their first visit to my office, I saw a couple who looked like a hundred couples I had seen before. They walked into the room, sat down, and looked straight ahead. Laura played nervously with the pillows on the sofa, while Sam alternated between crossing his legs and uncrossing them. It didn't take long to get the couple to open up.

"It's our marriage," Laura began. "Sam isn't giving it the attention it deserves, and I feel cheated."

As I turned to Sam, I received his view of the situation. "I work hard at my job," he said. "When I get home at night, I like things a certain way. Laura is going through this stage where she wants her independence in a big way. I can't really deal with it at this point in my life. It's her fault for changing so radically in the last three years. I shouldn't be expected to change that much!"

Like so many couples in their late thirties and early forties, this pair was going through a very difficult stage in their lives as individuals and as a couple. Laura was attempting to exercise some personal desires that she had buried for the last fifteen years of her life. Meanwhile, Sam was entering a time of life where he craved the "cocoon" of their home. These two agendas were colliding head-on. My assignment was to help this couple walk together again on the same path.

As we talked further, we discovered that Sam and Laura, like a lot of married couples, believed a lot of lies. When the truth finally comes to these couples, their choice is either to ask God for help to grow in their love or cling to the lies while the marriage slowly crumbles.

Marriage is hard work. Now that's a truth. Yet romantic notions blind couples to that truth, so they live with heartbreaking pain and misery.

The lies we'll be discussing in this chapter are not lies most married couples could consciously admit to believing, which makes confronting the lies much more difficult. Let's examine six of the most destructive lies couples believe.

IT'S ALL YOUR FAULT

One of the lies couples frequently believe is a form of the "It's somebody else's fault" lie, which points the finger of blame squarely at the marriage partner. It implies that the actions of one spouse make the other spouse react in a bad way, which is what makes the marriage rotten. Simply put, it's all his or her fault.

Sam was guilty of this thinking. He was telling me that the marital problems were all Laura's fault because she was changing. If she were like she used to be, everything would be just fine. He was okay. *She* was the one with the problem.

Is this a tendency in your life? Take a minute to honestly answer these questions. Circle your answer.

Do you see yourself as the cause of your unhappiness?

Yes   *No*

Do you avoid answering for your own actions?

Yes   *No*

Is your sense of personal worth improved by recognizing someone else's flaws?

Yes   *No*

Are you a person who habitually blames others?

Yes   *No*

Did you answer "Yes" to most of the questions? We all blame others to a certain extent, but we're looking at some serious patterning here. Do you remember the old cliché, "It takes two to tango"? It really does! It takes two people to create a horrible fight and two people to create a horrible marriage. Even when it seems that one person is "messing things up," I still would argue that the "offended" spouse's response to what the other spouse is doing is just as important to marital harmony.

Let's say Laura made her initial attempt at independence by announcing to Sam, "I'm sick and tired of being cooped up in this house, taking care of everybody else! It's time to take care of *me!* I'm going out and finding a job or some new friends or whatever it takes to get some sanity. I don't know when I'll be back—I might not come back. Deal with it!"

Sam could have responded in one of the following ways.

The "Put-Down" Response

Sam could have fired back, "Oh, that's brilliant, Einstein! Throw up your hands and just walk away! That's just like you, only thinking of yourself! You are selfish and stupid!"

Laura's response, like anyone else's, is to lash back defensively, that is, if she doesn't run out of the room, slamming the door behind her.

The "Keeping the Peace" Response

"Uhmm, well . . . that's great! I hope you'll find what it is you're looking for," Sam mumbles as he grips the kitchen counter hard enough to break a knuckle.

Laura's response, though, might be, "Good! I'm outta here! And I may be outta here for good!"

The "Speak the Truth in Love" Response

"I know how important independence is to you. And I know you've felt totally smothered lately. But do you really want to run away and not come back? That's not going to help you or us. Let's talk about how to make this work."

Laura's response? If Sam has made a habit of such reasonable responses, Laura might answer like this: "I'll be happy to discuss this with you. I want both of us to feel good about what I am doing. This can be a very positive thing."

Obviously, the third response is the healthiest one. No blame is being thrown around, and Sam and Laura are still communicating. It may sound somewhat idealistic, but I think communication like that is possible between couples if they work hard enough.

Suppose your spouse comes to you with some news that

startles you. You don't agree with the conclusions being drawn, but you are now in the situation where you must respond. Which of the responses characterizes you *in general?* Check one.

☐ The "Put-Down" Response
☐ The "Keeping the Peace" Response
☐ The "Speak the Truth in Love" Response

There is an important biblical truth at issue here. Read these words from the gospel of Matthew:

"Why do you look at the speck of sawdust in your brother's eye and pay no attention to the plank in your own eye?"

Matthew 7:3, NIV

We cannot see the speck in our mate's eye when we have a blinding plank in our own. Can you imagine a marriage in which each spouse puts this teaching into practice?

If this is an area of struggle in your marriage, take a few minutes to walk through the TRUTH system in the spaces that follow.

Trigger Event: _____

_____

_____

_____

Reckless Thinking: _____

_____

_____

_____

Unhealthy Reaction: _____

_____

_____

_____

Truthful Thinking: _____

_____

_____

Healthy Reaction: _____

_____

_____

_____

IF IT TAKES HARD WORK, WE MUST NOT BE RIGHT FOR EACH OTHER

Sam and Laura bought into this lie in their marriage. At the beginning of the chapter, I mentioned one of Sam's comments: "I work hard at my job. When I get home at night, I like things a certain way." Sam is illustrating a very common behavior, resulting from this lie. The implication of Sam's statement is that since he works hard all day at his job, the time he spends at home should be easy, enjoyable, and work-free. This attitude certainly is understandable, but it's just not the way things go. It's the fairy-tale mentality of finding the right person and "living happily ever after."

In countless counseling sessions with couples, I've seen this lie rear its ugly head. They think they married the wrong person because it takes so much hard work to keep everything together. It's just not like they thought it would be.

As strange as it sounds, I'd argue that hard work in marriage often suggests you married the right person. Overall, the difficult struggles in our marriages often show us where our own personalities are deficient and give us the chance to clean up our act.

Let's take a closer look at your personal situation.

Do you feel that you must work hard in your marriage? (Circle one.)

Yes   *No*

Much of our perception is based on how we compare with other couples. Compared to the couples you know, do you work harder than they do at their marriages, or do you see yourself not working as hard as they do, or is it about the same?

☐ *Work harder*
☐ *The same*
☐ *Not as hard*

What types of activities do you consider "work" in your marriage? *(For instance, "We have to work at talking with each other," or "We have to work at a satisfying sexual relationship.")*

_____

_____

_____

_____

Is the present stage of your marriage demanding more work than previous stages, or less work, or about the same?

☐ *More work*
☐ *About the same*
☐ *Less work*

Do you get discouraged about your marriage? Do you find yourself wanting to get out of it and look for a different partner? How often do you experience these feelings? (Circle one.)

Often
Sometimes
Never

My personal belief is that you can find maximum personal growth in your present marriage. The pursuit of a "new, improved" spouse is usually an escapist fantasy. The odds are you'd end up marrying someone who wasn't better for you at all, and maybe even worse. The painful truth is that marriage brings out areas of our lives we need to work on. You'd just be taking the same flaws into your next marriage.

When the apostle Paul commented on marriage, he observed:

> But those who marry will face many troubles in this life, and I want to spare you this.
>
> I Corinthians 7:28*b*, NIV

Have you had struggles in this area? Have you bought into this lie? Once again, use the TRUTH system to help you work through the proper thinking in this area.

Trigger Event: _____

_____

_____

_____

Reckless Thinking: _____

_____

_____

_____

Unhealthy Reaction: _____

_____

_____

_____

Truthful Thinking: _____

_____

_____

_____

Healthy Reaction: _____

_____

_____

_____

YOU CAN AND SHOULD MEET ALL MY NEEDS

"He's always been my white knight," is how Barbara began. "I could always count on Gary to be there. He did everything for me . . . gladly . . . never a complaint . . . never a problem."

"So what's wrong?" I asked.

"He's changed," Barbara replied. "He's not as available as he used to be. And when he is around, I hear him saying more and more that he can't do stuff for me and that I should do things myself. That's so unlike Gary. I'm really scared."

"What are you scared of?"

"I'm scared that he is losing interest in me. I'm afraid he is going to leave me."

"How would you feel if Gary left you?" I inquired.

"I would be devastated," Barbara whispered.

"Why?"

"Gary is my whole life," she confessed. "I don't have any friends. My extended family is all very distant from me. Any hobbies or interests are all wrapped around my husband." She paused and then added, "I guess that says something, doesn't it?"

Barbara had made an important discovery about herself. It is a very unhealthy situation to be in when you center your entire life around one person or thing. Not only is it extremely imbalanced, but it would also be "devastating" as Barbara put it, if that person or thing was no longer in your life. It would hurt.

Barbara believed the lie that Gary should meet all her needs. The reality of any relationship is that no one person can be the perfect "need meeter" for another person, so our needs are best met through a variety of healthy, appropriate sources.

Answer the following questions from your own life's experience.

Do you have hobbies that meet needs in your life? List them: *(For instance, "I enjoy going to garage sales with my friends early on Saturday mornings.")*

_____

_____

_____

How does your job fulfill some of your needs? *(For instance, "I use a great deal of creativity in my job, so it fulfills that need.")*

_____

_____

_____

Who are your friends, and what are the needs they meet in your life? *(For instance, "I have a friend who likes to play racquetball twice a week at the gym, thus meeting my need for some physical exercise.")*

_____

_____

_____

How would you describe your relationship with God, and how does it meet needs in your life? *(For instance, "I try to spend a little time each day reading a portion of the Bible, and, in doing so, I gain a better understanding of who I am from God's point of view.")*

_____

_____

_____

Don't underestimate the value of your relationship with God. Paul encouraged the believers in Philippi with the following words:

And my God will meet all your needs according to his glorious riches in Christ Jesus.

Philippians 4:19, NIV

Take a minute to memorize this passage of the New Testament.

Here is a three phase strategy to work through this issue. Think about these phases and assess where you are in each area.

1. Examine honestly what you expect from your spouse.

_____

_____

_____

_____

2. Examine honestly whether he or she can or will meet those needs.

_____
_____
_____
_____

3. Determine either to get the need met in an appropriate way through some other means, or accept that the need is inappropriate and work to give it up.

_____
_____
_____
_____

No one person can meet all our needs. Our spouses need to be let off the hook if that is what we are expecting from them. Think of an example of your spouse's not meeting a need and run it through the TRUTH system once again.

Trigger Event: _____
_____
_____
_____

Reckless Thinking: _____
_____
_____
_____

Unhealthy Reaction: _____
_____
_____
_____

Truthful Thinking: _____

_____

_____

_____

Healthy Reaction: _____

_____

_____

_____

YOU OWE ME

Somewhere between the magic world of dating and the real-life world of marriage comes the lie, "You owe me." It is a very common view in marriage that puts an emotional stranglehold on your relationship.

Darryl and Lynn struggle with this lie. Darryl works hard at his vocation, and as a result, is very successful. Lynn has opted to stay at home. When Darryl was studying for his master's degree, Lynn willingly worked part-time to help with finances. These days, unfortunately, Darryl's being selfish.

"Since I work my head off every day at the office," Darryl began, "all I want is for Lynn to return the favor by doing some of the things I want her to do."

Lynn bristled at his words. "He feels that I owe him. I just don't like the sound of that phrase."

Have you ever had these feelings? It's not uncommon for couples to "keep score" in their marriages. But even though it is common, it is damaging.

Try to imagine a radically different approach to your marriage. What if you take the point of view that your spouse owes you absolutely nothing for all the things you've done for him or her? You have done what you have done in the marriage because you chose to, not because you had to, and no one owes you anything for doing what you chose to do.

Take it a step further. What if you take the point of view that when your spouse does anything in return for what you've done for him or her, it is because *your spouse* has chosen to, not because your spouse has to. And what if you look upon what your spouse offers you as something to be accepted and appreciated instead of *expected?*

What I am proposing is this: Marriages get a lot healthier when you give up your *expectations* of each other and replace them with *wants* that, if not met, you meet in other appropriate ways.

I am not suggesting that in giving up expectations we should quit *wanting* or *desiring* things from our spouses. I *want* my wife to be loving, remain faithful, help me around the house, and keep a balanced checkbook. I'm just suggesting that she doesn't *owe* me those things, even if I provide them for her. The minute I start demanding these things from her as if they were my marital "birthright," I am believing my lie tape and will quickly fail to appreciate what she does offer me.

This is a tough question, but it must be asked: Exactly what do you expect from your mate? Jot down your thoughts.

_____

_____

_____

_____

_____

_____

From your list, what do you consider expectations and what are desires? Divide the list in the following spaces.

Expectations	*Desires*
_____	_____
_____	_____
_____	_____
_____	_____
_____	_____

So what do you do when you've given up expectations, but still don't get what you want? What terms best describe your style? Check all that are appropriate.

- ☐ Yell
- ☐ Withdraw
- ☐ Demean
- ☐ Manipulate
- ☐ Intimidate
- ☐ Ask your spouse to reconsider
- ☐ Flex
- ☐ Compromise
- ☐ Give up wanting it
- ☐ Look for some other way God can meet your need without your being bitter

Obviously the first half of that list is a group of unhealthy responses, whereas the last half is a list of healthy choices. The truth is that spouses "owe" each other nothing in marriage. The healthiest marriages are those in which each spouse gives because it is right to do so, not because it is owed or to be owed something in return.

I SHOULDN'T HAVE TO CHANGE

Sam and Laura, the couple at the beginning of this chapter, were going through their own version of this lie. Sam was especially upset at the changes that he saw in his home life. Laura was at the age where she was going through some dramatic changes. Unfortunately, Sam was not prepared for these changes. "I didn't sign on for all this change in our marriage," he commented. "I was perfectly content with the way things were. This is not my idea of a positive move in our relationship."

Since that was Sam's position, he was quite unwilling to accommodate Laura's needs. Put in simpler terms, Sam wouldn't change.

"This is the way I am," he would counter. "This is the way I've always been. I can't do anything about it. If Laura really loved me, she'd just accept me for what I am and not try to change me."

Can you identify with Sam? Have you felt your spouse would be happier in the relationship if you were willing and able to do some changing? For some of you, you can think of one or two areas where this might apply. For others, you can fill a list with potential changes! What sorts of changes has your spouse indicated that would be beneficial in your marriage? List them.

1. _____
2. _____
3. _____
4. _____
5. _____
6. _____

More often than not, our weaknesses are our spouse's strengths. Do you see this in your marriage? Jot down some weaknesses and strengths that come to mind.

My weaknesses

1. _____
2. _____
3. _____
4. _____

My mate's strengths

1. _____
2. _____
3. _____
4. _____

My strengths

1. _____
2. _____
3. _____
4. _____

My mate's weaknesses

1. _____
2. _____
3. _____
4. _____

Read what God said in the very beginning of time:

For this reason a man will leave his father and mother and be united to his wife, and they will become one flesh.

Genesis 2:24, NIV

What do you think God means when He uses the term *one flesh?*

_____
_____
_____

Becoming *one* is impossible if one or both spouses refuse to change for each other. I'm all for individuality, and I don't condone blind conformity to whatever a marriage partner wants just to make him or her happy. But when my wife is strong where I am not, it makes sense for me to move in her direction as much as I can, and vice versa. With that kind of mentality, both of us win because both of us become more complete—while we are becoming *one*. How does your understanding of *one flesh* go along with the need to be growing, maturing, and changing in your marriage?

_____

_____

_____

People who refuse to change end up stagnating and, in doing so, limit their opportunities for growth. The writer to the Hebrews stated it in beautiful simplicity:

> Make every effort to live in peace with all men and to be holy; without holiness no one will see the Lord.
>
> Hebrews 12:14, NIV

Relationships require change. A person's efforts to change someone else are most likely to end in frustration, even if successful. An effort to change yourself is more likely to be successful. Are there ways you could be "living in peace" with your spouse that you've previously resisted? Jot them down.

_____

_____

_____

Let's not forget the TRUTH system. Is there a trigger event that prompts this lie to surface in your life? Work through the process.

Trigger Event: _____

_____

_____

_____

Reckless Thinking: _____

_____

_____

_____

Unhealthy Reaction: _____

_____

_____

_____

Truthful Thinking: _____

_____

_____

_____

Healthy Reaction: _____

_____

_____

_____

YOU SHOULD BE LIKE ME

This lie is a second cousin to the previous lie and is much like the "My Way" lie we already looked at. The belief is that your own personal style is the "best" style and that your spouse must think, feel, and act like you in order to be right or acceptable. People who fall into this lie tend to see the world in black or white, right or wrong, all or nothing terms. They often arrogantly assume that because they think or feel or act a certain way their spouses are wrong if they don't think or feel or act the very same way. In blunt terms, such people want a clone more than a partner, whether they see it that way or not.

Does this lie crop up in your life? Put a check mark next to any of the following characteristics that describe common tendencies in your life.

- ☐ My way is best.
- ☐ My way is smartest.
- ☐ My way is most accurate.
- ☐ Because I think or act a certain way, anyone else is wrong if they differ.
- ☐ Everything is black or white.
- ☐ Everything is right or wrong.
- ☐ It's all or nothing.

Candice struggles with this lie. She grew up in a home where her parents doted over her and pretty much gave her whatever she asked for. When she met and married Art, she felt he would take care of her in the very same way. Now that they've been married long enough to have disagreements, Candice is beside herself over Art's "audacity" to express his own opinion, even when it differs from hers. It's a tough issue between the two of them.

It sounds childish, but they often argue over what restaurant to visit on their Friday night "date." If Art doesn't agree with Candice's choice, she will fall into a silent, passive rage or explode in a fury. Lately, there have been quite a few Friday nights when they stayed home because they couldn't agree on a restaurant, and Candice didn't want to go out with such an uncooperative man!

At the heart of this issue is the ability to accept differences. If we were married to someone who felt and acted exactly the way we did, we'd be bored within a week. Differences are a vital part in any relationship. The New Testament teaches us:

But in fact God has arranged the parts in the body, every one of them, just as he wanted them to be. If they were all one part, where would the body be? As it is, there are many parts, but one body.

1 Corinthians 12:18–20, NIV

Go back to the previous lie and review your strengths and weaknesses, as well as the strengths and weaknesses of your mate. Can you see the distinct advantage of differences in your particular situation?

We are unique. It's good that we are all different, even if it does lead to conflict, because maturely handled differences can give us a clearer sense of our own individuality, a greater appreciation for how different human beings really are, and motivation to make needed changes.

Is there a particular circumstance that brings out this lie in your life? Jot it down as the trigger event, and proceed through the TRUTH system to its healthy conclusion.

Trigger Event: _____

_____

_____

_____

Reckless Thinking: _____

_____

_____

_____

Unhealthy Reaction: _____

_____

_____

_____

Truthful Thinking: _____

_____

_____

_____

Healthy Reaction: _____

_____

_____

_____

LOOKING OVER
WHERE WE'VE BEEN

This has been an important chapter in that it has covered lies that affect more than our personal, individual life—they affect our most significant human relationship, our marriage. Instead of a review that takes us back through the material in an academic sense, let's end this chapter on a very practical note. Review your notes in this section and answer the following questions.

Which of these six lies do you struggle with the most? (Check one.)

☐ It's all your fault.

☐ If it takes hard work, we must not be right for each other.

☐ You can and should meet all my needs.

☐ You owe me.

☐ I shouldn't have to change.

☐ You should be like me.

Now, take what you have learned about defeating that particular lie and apply it to your marriage. What can you do *now*, to put this into practice? Choose one of the following ideas as a starter in your application of the truth.

- Write your mate a love letter.
- Take your mate out for a date.
- Go for a long walk and talk.
- Pick his/her favorite restaurant and have a leisurely meal together.
- Send your mate flowers or a favorite gift.
- Farm out the kids and enjoy a quiet evening at home.
- Send your mate a card with a loving sentiment in it.
- Arrange for a weekend getaway and do it!
- Call your mate at home or at work just to be thoughtful.
- Do something totally out of character for your spouse—be creative!
- Apologize for something you did or said that was wrong—regardless of what part your spouse played in the incident.

GROUP DISCUSSION STARTERS

1. Why do we tend to blame others? Share a personal example of the "Put-Down" response or the "Keeping the Peace" response or the "Speak the Truth in Love" response.

2. How has our culture contributed to the lie that marriage shouldn't be hard work? How do you teach this concept to your children? How have the current trends toward quick and easy divorce entered into this equation?

3. Perhaps someone in your group can share how he or she was personally affected by the lie, "You can and should meet all my needs." Is the modern view of romance at work here? How can we balance the White Knight and Lovely Princess with reality?

4. The "You Owe Me" lie speaks a great deal about expectations. What expectations did you bring into your marriage that

had to be adjusted? How do you distinguish between desires and expectations in your marriage? What advice would you give younger couples on dealing with expectations?

5. Why are humans so resistant to change? What is the most radical change you've had to make in your marriage? What was the most difficult change your spouse had to make in order to live at peace with you?

6. Differences provide a broader base in our marriages. Every person in the group probably has a humorous story of how differences provided for some crazy moments at home. If they are not too embarrassing, share them with one another. What is the most important lesson you have learned about being a unique creation of God?

7. Spend some time with your buddy catching up on what has been going on in his/her life. Check in on any new prayer requests, and get updated on the ones you've been praying about. What did this chapter's material bring to light that is on the forefront of your thinking this week? How can you help your buddy process this material? Make sure you switch roles so that you can talk about your situation as well.

Chapter 6

DEFEATING DISTORTION LIES

When was the last time you blew up over something small?

Do you take things too personally?

How often do you use the words *always* and *never?*

Do you base your actions on feelings more than facts?

Be honest. How did you answer those questions? Each one concerns a distortion. We often distort reality. That practice is the foundation for most of our lies. Some of these distortions are quite familiar in themselves, and they foster their own familiar false ideas.

The truth is that everybody falls into these distortions. They're a part of most people's normal thinking. Each distortion, though, contributes to our misery and immaturity and needs to be exposed. Let's look at these distortions one at a time.

A MOUNTAIN OUT OF A MOLEHILL

Gary was beside himself. All he could do was stare at his watch and fume. "He's already fifteen minutes late!" he groaned.

Gary had been seated at the restaurant for twenty-five minutes. He was almost always on time and often, as in this case, early.

"Are you ready to order, sir?" the waiter asked.

"No!" snapped Gary. "I'm waiting for my associate, and he's very late!"

The waiter left, deeply offended.

When Charlie showed up, Gary was ready for him. "Well, well, well. Look who decided to finally show up!"

"I'm so sorry I'm late, Gary," Charlie apologized. "Traffic was terrible."

"I don't want to hear it," Gary snapped back. "All I know is I've been sitting here for thirty minutes and you've inconvenienced me. I thought you were more responsible than this, Charlie."

Charlie sat in stunned silence. "I was late for lunch. Aren't you overreacting a bit?"

"Oh, that just tops it off!" Gary barked. "I've had enough. I'm outta here." And with that, Gary walked out in a huff, leaving Charlie shaking his head in utter disbelief.

Gary is suffering from a distortion called *magnification*. In this distortion, an event is made much bigger than it is in reality. Gary made a mountain out of a molehill. By taking what Charlie did (or didn't do) and making it into a bigger situation than it really was, Gary was lying to himself. And by lying to himself, he turned up the volume on his emotions.

Is this an issue in your life? Do you practice your own version of magnification? Look at the list that follows. Do you overreact to any of these situations? If so, put a check mark beside the situation.

☐ Driving in traffic

☐ Waiting on people who are late

☐ Coping with clutter or mess at home or work

☐ Waiting in line

☐ Talking to telephone salespeople
☐ Dealing with incompetence
☐ Handling teenagers
☐ Being stood up for an appointment
☐ Sitting through sermons that run too long on Sundays
☐ Receiving your paycheck a day later than usual

Did any of those yank your chain? Take a few minutes to recall the TRUTH system. Any one of the situations in the list could be characterized as a trigger event. How you react is based on believing truth or lies. For instance, if you feel the pastor went over his allotted time in his Sunday sermon, and if you buy into the distortion of magnification, that reckless thinking will cause you to react in an unhealthy manner. You may lose your temper, raise your blood pressure, or take out your frustration on your spouse or children. What you need is a dose of truthful thinking. A sermon can run overtime without serious implications to the future of the world. It's no big deal, is it? When you expose this trigger event to truthful thinking, a healthy reaction will result.

Put one of your sample trigger events through the TRUTH system. Follow it through to its conclusion.

Trigger Event: _____

_____

_____

_____

Reckless Thinking: _____

_____

_____

_____

Unhealthy Reaction: _____

_____

_____

_____

Truthful Thinking: _____

_____

_____

_____

Healthy Reaction: _____

_____

_____

_____

TAKING EVERYTHING PERSONALLY

"Ben doesn't love me anymore. I'm certain of it." These words came from a somber wife named Heidi one day in a session.

"How do you know this?" I asked.

"It's obvious," she replied. "He treats me with no respect."

"Give me some examples," I pressed.

"Well, for starters, he's a slob," she muttered. "He constantly leaves clothes all over the house, assuming I will pick them up. When I try to talk to him about it, he seems to avoid the issue. He tells me that's just the way he is, but I think there's more to it than that. I think he's lashing out at me, and I'm very hurt by it."

"How long has Ben been leaving his clothes around the house?" I inquired. "Is this something new?"

"Actually, he's been sloppy for years," Heidi admitted.

"How many years?" I asked.

She paused, then spoke through clenched teeth, "I guess he's been this way as long as I've known him."

"So it's not a new behavior," I commented.

"Okay, maybe not, but still, he's angry at me, I just know it. He wouldn't be this inconsiderate for any other reason."

"Is it possible that Ben's personality is that of a guy who tends to be more creative and spontaneous rather than neat and organized?" I inquired.

"Ben is a highly creative man," Heidi answered. "That's one of the qualities that attracted me to him."

"Then it must also be possible that Ben's leaving his clothes around the house is not to be taken as a personal assault on you, right?"

"I guess that's possible," Heidi whispered.

"Perhaps you're personalizing something that isn't personal," I commented.

Heidi's reaction to Ben's lack of neatness is a style of distorting called *personalization*. In this distortion, the person overestimates the extent an event relates to him or her. *Everything is personal.*

This is an issue that comes up a great deal between couples. Do you see this in your relationship? Can you list some examples of situations where personalization comes into play? *(For instance, he/she never wants to talk, he/she drinks too much, he/she stays out at meetings too late, he/she never takes me seriously, he/she never wears the slacks I bought him/her.)*

I'm not suggesting that we should react with indifference to what our spouses do or that their behavior is totally unrelated to how they feel toward us. I'm only suggesting that our tendency to take what they do personally makes us overreact, which makes the situation worse. Not only is the original problem still intact, but we add unnecessary anger, resentment, and bitterness to the mess.

Now review the list you just made and answer the following question: Could there be other reasons for this behavior? If so, jot them down.

_____

_____

_____

_____

_____

In reality, what other people do says much more about them than you. What can you learn from these situations about the other person? *(For instance, "My mate's inability to get home from work on time is a sign of workaholism—he's trying to prove something to his boss.")*

_____

_____

_____

_____

In my counseling experience, situations such as Ben and Heidi's don't get better until hurt feelings are faced, until the focus is more on who Ben is—what makes him do what he does—than on how it affects Heidi personally. Almost without exception, when the discussion turns to the real reasons for the other person's behavior, the offended person begins to see that he or she is not the true reason for the other person's actions at all.

If you wrestle with the lie of taking everything personally, pick a sample trigger event and walk through the TRUTH system.

Trigger Event: _____

_____

_____

_____

Reckless Thinking: _____

_____

_____

_____

Unhealthy Reaction: _____

_____

_____

_____

Truthful Thinking: _____

_____

_____

_____

Healthy Reaction: _____

_____

_____

_____

EVERYTHING IS BLACK/WHITE

"Everything is either black or white to you!"

Ever had this criticism thrown your way? If so, you are being accused of a style of distorted thinking called *polarization*, which takes reality and cuts it into black and white—all or nothing—extremes.

If you polarize, you often react to things with either a "That was great!" or "That was awful!" gut feeling. You lump people into good and bad categories. Politicians, for instance, either elicit your admiration or your loathing. This style of thinking doesn't allow you to see the gray areas of life, much less appreciate them. And when turned inward, such polarized thinking brings severe emotional fallout.

One of the more serious "inward" forms of polarized thinking is "scum/saint" thinking. This is where you view yourself as either completely scummy or completely saintly, or you flip back and forth between the two.

Do you struggle in this area? If so, which side of the polarization spectrum do you favor, saint or scum?

How did this happen? What effect did the following groups have on your development of this thinking?

Your parents: *(For instance, "They always told me I was no good, so I felt like scum.")*

_____

_____

_____

_____

Your siblings: *(For instance, "My younger sisters adored me— they believed I could do no wrong.")*

_____

_____

_____

Your teachers: *(For instance, "I was always put in the slow groups in grade school and made to feel stupid.")*

_____

_____

_____

_____

Your church: *(For instance, "I grew up thinking I had to be perfect in order to gain God's love and approval.")*

_____

_____

_____

_____

Your society: *(For instance, "I grew up thinking only the beautiful people mattered, and I felt ugly, thus, no good to anyone.")*

_____

_____

_____

_____

The truth is, you are a blend of both saintly qualities and scummy ones, too. It's not until we get a grasp on both sides of this issue that we can experience real emotional growth. Are you ready for an honest assessment of both sides of your life?

What are the positive, "saintly" qualities in your life? *(For instance, "I am a committed, faithful spouse," "I am a loving parent," "I am a hard worker.")*

_____

_____

_____

_____

What are some negative or "scummy" characteristics with which you struggle? *(For instance, "I constantly battle with overeat-*

ing," "I struggle with lust," "I can be very lazy," "I can say very unkind things to people.")

_____

_____

_____

_____

Each list should be about equal in length. If it's not, there's a clue that you tend to polarize.

Obviously, there are certain issues that *are* black or white, and we need to view them that way. The existence of God, for example, is a black or white issue in my opinion. He either exists or He does not exist. Jesus Christ, then, was either God incarnate or He was not. Sins against society, such as murder or stealing, are also black or white matters. I don't think we can afford to be gray about them, do you?

Those are some examples of black or white issues for me. What about you? What are some examples of black or white issues in your thinking? List them.

_____

_____

_____

_____

The polarized thinker takes all of life and forces it into a black or white format. When the issues faced are black or white, there is no problem. When the issues are gray, though, as many are, polarized thinking creates needless emotional distress. The challenge is to be flexible enough to read the "shade" of a situation properly, reading black as black, white as white, and the in-between as its appropriate shade of gray. We need to use good judgment and discern issues of "shade" more accurately.

If you are a polarizer, take an incident that best represents this struggle, write it down as a trigger event, and work it through the TRUTH system.

Trigger Event: _____

_____

_____

_____

Reckless Thinking: _____

_____

_____

_____

Unhealthy Reaction: _____

_____

_____

_____

Truthful Thinking: _____

_____

_____

_____

Healthy Reaction: _____

_____

_____

_____

MISSING THE FOREST FOR THE TREES

A good friend of mine shared an interesting story with me over lunch one day. He had just returned from a business meeting in another city, and he was telling me all about the speaker he had heard at this convention.

"Chris, this guy was fabulous!" he exclaimed. "You know me, I'm not one to dole out praise unless it's earned. Believe me, this guy earned it!"

He shared a little more about the speaker and his topic, and then he made a fascinating observation. "I did something I don't normally do. I went up to the platform after this guy's speech to thank him for doing such a good job. Well, there was a line of people all waiting to do the same. I waited and watched as one by one, the people thanked this man. But, at one point, a woman began to express her dismay on how he covered one aspect of his topic. Chris, this guy went into a tailspin! He pulled the lady out of line and talked with her for thirty-five minutes. His assistant was standing right there, so I asked him what was going on. He said, 'This is pretty common. When someone doesn't like his speech, it totally discounts everyone else's positive comments. He'll stew over this lady's gripe for a month!'"

This is an offshoot of the polarization lie. It's called *selective abstraction*. It's the "can't see the forest for the trees" distortion. In spite of all the positive responses the speaker received, he could only focus on the negative one.

Do you feel this struggle in particular areas of your life?

Do you "miss the forest for the trees" in any of these areas?

At home: *(For instance, you may spend all day cleaning the house, but at the end of the day you only see what you didn't do.)*

_____

_____

_____

At work: *(For instance, you work on a report all day. The content is excellent, but you can't get past the typo on page sixteen.)*

_____

_____

_____

In your parenting: *(For instance, you ignore your child when the child is behaving, but pay attention to the child's misbehavior.)*

_____

_____

_____

In your hobbies: *(For instance, in your tennis game, you hit ten good shots and one bad one, and you dwell on the bad one.)*

_____

_____

_____

In your spiritual life: *(For instance, when you read your Bible, you only pay attention to verses that concern judgment or sin or works while ignoring verses on grace or forgiveness—or vice versa.)*

_____

_____

_____

I can't overemphasize how important it is to get a handle on this lie. Many psychiatric patients are in the hospital partly because of their tendency to focus on what is bad rather than on what is good. It's as if they have on a pair of "deficiency" glasses, which allow only the bad to come through. And you can count on it, when you only see the bad, depression is close behind.

Perhaps as you reflected on the different areas of your life, you saw the lie at work within you. You're probably getting used to the TRUTH system by now, but don't allow familiarity to take away its powerful effect on you. The truth is important!

Trigger Event: _____
_____
_____
_____

Reckless Thinking: _____
_____
_____
_____

Unhealthy Reaction: _____
_____
_____
_____

Truthful Thinking: _____
_____
_____
_____

Healthy Reaction: _____
_____
_____
_____

HISTORY ALWAYS REPEATS ITSELF

"We never get along with each other!" Cheryl lamented to me in the office one day. "Stan just wears me out. He listens to my arguments about a particular issue, then he starts to put me down. I can't seem to stand up for myself, so he always wins!"

The more I talked to Cheryl, the more I understood her situation. Her twelve-year marriage to Stan had fallen into a pattern of criticizing and nitpicking, which ensures they will never be happy with each other. The interesting thing about Cheryl's attitude is how she freely used the words *always* and *never* to describe their situation.

These two words are the keys to a style of distorted thinking called *overgeneralization*. In this distortion, any event or behavior, such as eating a Twinkie, failing an exam, or fighting with a spouse, leads to the lie that the future will inescapably hold more of the same. History, supposedly, *always* repeats itself.

Do you use the words *always* and *never* frequently? If so, in what sorts of situations? Check the ones that apply.

☐ Conversing with your spouse
☐ Struggling with a personal habit
☐ Accomplishing a particular goal
☐ Performing at your job
☐ Relating with your kids
☐ Working at your hobby
☐ Relating with your parents
☐ Learning a new task
☐ Volunteering at church activities
☐ Other: _____

It isn't uncommon for many of my clients to overgeneralize about their mental health. They often fear that they will never get better. When they conclude this, they typically keep the same self-defeating styles of thinking and acting that made them troubled in the first place. My response is to push them to see each day as a unique opportunity to turn events around. They often fight me on this, but it would be very difficult for them to improve when they are feeling doomed to repeat the mistakes and pain of the past.

Why do you think it is so easy to believe that history must repeat itself? Look at the following statements and circle whether you agree or disagree with each statement.

1. The future will inescapably repeat what happened in the past.

Agree   *Disagree*

2. Things can never get better, they can only get worse.

Agree   *Disagree*

3. People tend to follow paths of habit and tradition.

Agree   *Disagree*

4. History repeating itself contains an element of truth.

Agree   *Disagree*

If there is one word to focus on in defeating this lie, it is the word *change*. Do you honestly believe change is possible in your life? Be assured by the words of the New Testament:

Therefore, if anyone is in Christ, he is a new creation; the old has gone, the new has come!
                              2 Corinthians 5:17, NIV

Have you ever thought of the stark contrast that is presented in that verse? The horrible old habits you brought along from your life before Christ are now open to change!

List some of your old habits that plague you.

_____

_____

_____

_____

_____

How can your life as a Christian bring about change in these areas?

_____

_____

_____

_____

_____

If you've never memorized this wonderful verse, do it now. What a great promise to rely on in times of struggle!

DON'T CONFUSE ME WITH THE FACTS

When Tim first walked into my office, I was stunned. Here was a guy who had success oozing out of his pores! Imagine my disbelief as he began to spill out his story.

"I'm a real mess," he began. "I know I appear successful to people around me, but the truth is, I am horribly insecure, and I feel like a big zero."

"Why do you feel this way?" I asked.

"Well, it goes back to when I was a child," Tim said in a soft voice. "I was really overweight as a kid. Who am I kidding? I was more than overweight—I was *fat!* All the kids made fun of me constantly. I couldn't play in their games because they would always choose sides and no one would pick me. I began to compensate by being the class clown. I was smart enough to know that no one would want to be around me since I was fat, so I became funny to be accepted by the group."

"And did you succeed in being accepted?"

"I guess. But I still felt like a nothing."

"You felt like you had to earn your place among your friends, didn't you?"

"Yeah, that's exactly how it felt."

"So go on with your story," I encouraged.

"I went off to college and I went through a major transition. I lost a lot of weight and began to take a little more pride in my appearance. The interesting thing that happened is that a lot of the social skills I developed as the little fat boy stayed with me, and I became quite popular on campus. Before I knew it, I was president of my class, and voted 'Most Likely to Succeed.'"

"And then?"

"And then I took the business world by storm!" he replied, excitement growing in his voice. "I met and married a beautiful young lady, started having babies, making money, and enjoying a status of life I had never had before. All along, I was grateful to God for all His blessings on me."

"It sounds pretty wonderful," I added.

"Yeah, I guess it is." He paused. "But I still can't get past the feelings of inadequacy and inferiority. I still feel like that little fat kid."

"So what you are saying is that you don't want to accept the facts."

"What do you mean?" he snapped back.

"All these facts you have presented me paint a pretty enviable picture, Tim. But you feel a different way; therefore, you are believing a distortion that says, 'Because I feel it to be true, it is true.' But it's not true. It's your feelings doing a number on you."

Tim was dealing with a lie. It's a distortion of the truth called *emotional reasoning*. Usually this is not a distorted style of thinking that we openly recognize. It is masked by other lies, making those lies *feel* like truths. Emotional reasoning can make feelings appear to be facts.

Feelings, though, are just feelings. They change quite a bit, they are hard to predict, and they often spring from irrational and unrealistic ways of thinking. Therefore, they often yield unreliable assessments of what the "facts" are. That's where the lie comes in.

Think back to the last time you had to make a major decision. Can you summarize the situation? *(For instance, "The washing machine broke down, and we had to decide whether to pay a large sum to fix it or buy a new one.")*

_____

_____

_____

_____

Was your decision-making process dominated by your feelings or the facts or a combination of both? Briefly explain what took place.

_____

_____

_____

_____

Unfortunately, when people turn their feelings into facts, they become much harder to help. Tim, for example, had turned his feelings of inferiority into fact, so he had locked himself into a position that made helping him almost impossible. After all, who can argue with "facts"?

This is more than an emotional issue; it is a spiritual one as well. We return to the all powerful spiritual concept of developing the mind of Christ. Paul, in his second letter to the Corinthians, wrote:

> We demolish arguments and every pretension that sets itself up against the knowledge of God, and we take captive every thought to make it obedient to Christ.
>
> 2 Corinthians 10:5, NIV

What does it mean to you to "take captive every thought to make it obedient to Christ"?

_____

_____

Can you rewrite that phrase in your own words, giving it personal meaning?

_____

_____

How can this verse help you defeat this lie in your life?

_____

_____

LOOKING OVER
WHERE WE'VE BEEN

Distortion lies can be very damaging in your life. Take a few minutes to look over the six lies we discussed. In the space provided, rewrite each lie in your own words, write down the truth that offsets the lie, and then write down the most important application you can make to your life.

A Mountain out of a Molehill

The lie: _____

_____

The truth: _____

_____

The application: _____

_____

Taking Everything Personally

The lie: _____

_____

The truth: _____

_____

The application: _____

_____

Everything Is Black/White

The lie: _____

_____

The truth: _____

_____

The application: _____

_____

Missing the Forest for the Trees

The lie: _____

_____

The truth: _____

_____

The application: _____

_____

History Always Repeats Itself

The lie: _____

_____

The truth: _____

_____

The application: _____

_____

Don't Confuse Me with the Facts

The lie: _____

_____

The truth: _____

_____

The application: _____

_____

GROUP DISCUSSION STARTERS

1. Have group members who are parents share some examples of how their kids made mountains out of molehills. Most likely, these stories will be pretty humorous—and pretty amazing!

2. Why are most of us unaware that there are alternative reasons for another person's behavior? Why do we tend to take everything so personally? What are some of your strategies to combat personalization?

3. Do you see any relation between the black/white lie and a person's level of maturity? Do you agree with the statement that very few of life's events are extreme?

4. Missing the forest for the trees often translates into seeing only the bad and overlooking the good. Why is this so damaging? How can we retrain ourselves to see the bigger picture?

5. How has your relationship with the Lord helped you to defeat the "History always repeats itself" lie? What does it really mean to you to be a "new creation" through Christ?

6. Are you better characterized as a "facts" person or a "feelings" person? How about your mate? Do opposites attract? Why do you think God created us with such strong feelings?

7. Meet with your buddy and share prayer requests. Check in with each other on the progress you're making and what you're learning through this study. Don't be in a hurry.

Chapter 7

DEFEATING RELIGIOUS LIES

We've been talking about defeating the lies in your life by replacing them with the truth. So far, we've seen lies we tell ourselves, lies we receive from the world, lies we believe in our marriages, and the lies of distortion. I call this section *religious* lies, and I believe these lies are the most resilient of all the categories we've discussed.

The reason I say that is because these lies are taught to us as God's beliefs. Any Christian would have a hard time giving them up, because to do so means, it seems, to directly disagree with God. It's a catch-22. If Christians keep believing these lies (which they actually see as truth), they stay spiritually and emotionally troubled, but if they dispute the lies, they feel they're displeasing God. Either way they go, they can't win.

But religious lies are like the other lies in several ways. Like other lies, they are emotionally damaging. And like other lies, they are rarely questioned. The Christian might know intellectually that such beliefs are untrue, but he or she still responds as if they are true.

Religious lies go a step further than other lies, however, because they make spiritual well-being almost impossible for the Christian who lives by them. It's tough. Without spiritual well-being, how can we be whole? The first step, as always, is to acknowledge these lies, so let's look at the most common religious lies my patients express.

GOD'S LOVE MUST BE EARNED

Suzanne was a pleaser. She did whatever it took to get people to like her. This was no more obvious than in her relationship with her parents. Suzanne was obsessed with earning the love of her mom and dad. As in many cases of this nature, her parents didn't really see this behavior as improper, so they actually encouraged it. Suzanne was as "perfect" as a little girl could be. Secretly, however, Suzanne felt horrible when she went through times of "not measuring up."

As you might expect, this sort of thinking spilled over into her beliefs about God. Suzanne concluded that God was exactly like her parents: God loved her, but it was in direct correlation to how she performed. God loved her more when she did good things, and God loved her less when she did bad things. God's love ran hot or cold, depending on the condition of her performance.

This kind of thinking fuels Christian perfectionism, which forces a person to live under the law rather than grace. Christians like Suzanne soon see God as constantly angry and disappointed with them.

Can you identify with these feelings? How do you see God in your life? Are you guilty of believing the "Earned Love" lie?

Here's an important place to start: Where and from whom

did you learn your beliefs and feelings about God? If you are like most people, you probably learned them from a variety of places and people. Take a few minutes to jot down the key concepts about God that you learned from these different sources. Include the truths you learned as well as the distortions.

What I learned about God from my parents: *(For instance, "I learned about accepting Jesus as my Savior as a little child, but I also learned the distortion that God would hate me if I misbehaved.")*

Truth: _____

_____

Distortion: _____

_____

What I learned about God from my Sunday school teachers as a child:

Truth: _____

_____

Distortion: _____

_____

What I learned about God from my church youth leaders:

Truth: _____

_____

Distortion: _____

_____

What I learned about God from my pastor:

Truth: _____

_____

Distortion: _____

_____

What I learned about God from friends:

Truth: _____

_____

Distortion: _____

_____

What I learned about God by myself:

Truth: _____

_____

Distortion: _____

_____

As adults, some of us acquire a more mature concept of God, while others stay stuck in their old view, and the lie that God's love must be earned festers.

Can God's love be earned?

Absolutely not.

Do many Christians feel and act as if it has to be earned?

Absolutely!

The primary challenge to the Christian battling this lie is to confront it, not with feelings, but with what Scripture says about the issue. Paul encouraged the believers in Rome to understand the truth when he wrote to them:

> But God demonstrates his own love for us in this: While we were still sinners, Christ died for us.
>
> Romans 5:8, NIV

God doesn't turn His back on us when we sin! Apparently the "Earned Love" lie was running around Ephesus as well. Paul wrote to them:

For it is by grace you have been saved, through faith—and this not from yourselves, it is the gift of God—not by works, so that no one can boast.

> Ephesians 2:8–9, NIV

Meditating on such statements that contradict the "God's love must be earned" lie is the first step toward acknowledging its falseness.

GOD HATES THE SIN AND THE SINNER

Harrison was an exceptionally good-looking man in his mid-forties. He explained to me that he had been a Christian for more than ten years. He was active in his church, a loving husband, and a caring dad. What prompted him to visit me was fascinating.

"I joined this small Bible study group sponsored by my church," Harrison said. "Like most new groups, we began by going around the room and sharing our testimonies—you know, how we came to accept Christ as Savior. Well, I don't know if it was God's version of a joke or what, but person after person shared his or her past, and I soon discovered all the people in the group were basically brought up in church. They had all received Christ as children. Some of them went through a brief period of rebellion—maybe as a teenager or in college—but, all in all, it's a pretty tame group."

"Please, go on with your story," I encouraged.

"When it came my turn to share my life, I suddenly felt very embarrassed. My story was very different from the others. I was a bad kid—I mean, a real bad kid. I was in a gang, I drank, I did drugs, I was arrested several times. I had a string of girlfriends that I just used for my own pleasure and then dumped. I beat on my younger brothers all the time. I guess you're getting the picture. You can imagine what a life-changing experience it was when I was introduced to the gospel! It totally changed my life to accept Christ. It's been amazing. I'm really grateful."

"So what brings you here?" I inquired.

"It's like this, Dr. Thurman. The whole experience of this small group made me realize how rotten I was. I've been kind of overwhelmed by it. I'm real sad, real depressed. I've started to doubt my relationship to God as being real."

"Why?"

"Because I feel I've done too many bad things for God to really love me. I know Christ died for sinners, but being in this group made me realize I'm a BAD sinner. I guess I never compared myself to others in this way before. I just can't see how God could love me."

Harrison's situation is an interesting one. Here is a man who understood the love of God, yet later in life became riddled with doubts because he started to accept the lie that "God must hate me because of all my sin." By the way, many times this thinking leads to self-hate, as well.

When we buy into this misconception, we make turning away from sin more difficult. Why? Because the energy it takes to turn from sin is used up by the self-hate we waste on ourselves. It mixes the emotional reasoning lie from the distortion chapter with a misunderstanding of God's true concept of confession and forgiveness. The worst part is that it is totally self-defeating—a vicious circle.

Does this lie find its way into your thinking? Why is it difficult to separate the sin from the sinner? Look at the following sentences, and put a check mark by any that you can relate to in your life.

- ☐ People are taught that when they *do* bad, they *are* bad.
- ☐ It is difficult for me to forgive myself, even after another person has forgiven me.
- ☐ It is difficult for me to accept God's forgiveness, since I can't forgive myself.

☐ I feel I must be punished for what I've done wrong.

☐ God's love is directly related to my doing right or wrong.

Once again, we need to confront this lie by contradicting it with the truth. Paul makes a statement that absolutely liberates the Christian!

Therefore, there is now no condemnation for those who are in Christ Jesus, because through Christ Jesus the law of the Spirit of life set me free from the law of sin and death.

Romans 8:1–2, NIV

What does it really mean to you to be set free from sin?

_____

_____

Does this mean *all* sin? (Circle one.)

       Yes   *No*

Does this include your most horrible sin?

       Yes   *No*

Do you believe that God has forgiven you?

       Yes   *No*

Are you willing to forgive yourself?

       Yes   *No*

Why or why not? _____

_____

_____

What is it about this issue that presents the biggest hurdle to overcome?

_____

_____

_____

_____

Do you have someone you can talk this over with? Who?

_____

Will you take some time to call that person and set up a meeting to discuss this? I hope you will. It would also be good for you to talk to God about it. Why not take a moment right now to pray. Ask God for His help in gaining victory in this battle. Thank Him for the truth. Confess your shortcomings in the past, and thank Him for His forgiveness.

In dealing with sin, God would have us correct the sin, then correct the damage we have done to others who've been affected by it, and finally dedicate ourselves to turning away from that sin in the future. Decide to do it God's way. It's the only way that promotes growth.

BECAUSE I'M A CHRISTIAN, GOD WILL PROTECT ME FROM PAIN AND SUFFERING

One of the most hotly debated issues in history has been the relation between God and human suffering. Who hasn't heard these types of statements down through the years?

"If God is a God of love, why is there human suffering?"

"God wants you healed. Just have faith."

"If you're hurting, there must be sin in your life."

"I became a Christian to be happy."

"God wants me healthy and wealthy."

"The Christian life is a problem-free life!"

Ever heard any of those? We all have our own versions of stories that relate back to this issue. Being a Christian means joy, peace, and contentment, we are told. We happily misconstrue that to mean a Christian never has problems or pain. We think we're protected so that we'll never lose our jobs, suffer from illness, or have accidents that happen to "other" people. This lie may be the most insidious religious falsehood in Christendom. Daily, hourly, people are hurt by it.

So how do we explain the truth? The truth, as we've discussed earlier, is that life is difficult. Faith makes it less difficult, not by rescuing us, but by giving us a resource to handle the problems.

Free will is the hub, I believe, of our daily living and hurting. At the risk of oversimplifying, I believe God has given us free will and will not get in the way of our using it. He will allow us to make unhealthy choices that bring us painful consequences. God will allow me, for example, to drive my car one hundred miles an hour; and He won't necessarily step in and prevent me from killing myself.

Perhaps a helpful exercise would be to develop a theology of suffering. It is a biblical teaching that Christians suffer. Read through the following verses. After you read each one, write it in your own words, and state what you believe to be the key kernel of doctrinal truth.

For it has been granted to you on behalf of Christ not only to believe on him, but also to suffer for him.

Philippians 1:29, NIV

Paraphrase: _____

_____

_____

Key truth: _____

_____

_____

It is better, if it is God's will, to suffer for doing good than for doing evil.

1 Peter 3:17, NIV

Paraphrase: _____

_____

_____

Key truth: _____

_____

_____

However, if you suffer as a Christian, do not be ashamed, but praise God that you bear that name.

1 Peter 4:16, NIV

Paraphrase: _____

_____

_____

Key truth: _____

_____

_____

And the God of all grace, who called you to his eternal glory in Christ, after you have suffered a little while, will himself restore you and make you strong, firm and steadfast.

1 Peter 5:10, NIV

Paraphrase: _____

_____

_____

Key truth: _____

_____

_____

Why is suffering part of God's plan? Look up the following references in your New Testament, and write a phrase or sentence for each. (My suggested answers appear below.)

1. Romans 5:3–5

_____

2. Romans 8:17–18

_____

3. 2 Corinthians 1:8–9

_____

4. 2 Timothy 1:11–12

_____

5. 1 Peter 1:6–7

_____

Why is suffering part of God's plan? Here are the answers I found in these verses:
1. Build character
2. Share in God's glory
3. Shift our dependence from ourselves to God
4. A part of ministry
5. Prove our faith to be genuine and receive praise, glory, and honor

Aristotle said, "We cannot learn without pain." This sums up a great truth, and we need to remember it in order to fight off the "God will protect me from pain and suffering" lie.

ALL MY PROBLEMS ARE CAUSED BY MY SINS

Do you remember Harrison from earlier in the chapter? He was struggling with his past—especially all the sins he committed before he came to Christ. As our sessions continued, he began to wrestle with a problem stemming from a related distortion of the truth.

"Things have really taken a turn for the worse," he told me one day. "Business is way down. It looks like we're going to lay off people." He paused. "I'm certain I'll be one of those who goes."

"Why are you certain?" I asked.

"Because of my sins," he concluded quietly. "God messes up our lives to punish us for our sins."

"So the only time people have problems is when they sin—is that what you are saying, Harrison?"

"Well, it may sound dumb to you, but it makes perfect sense to me!" was Harrison's deflated reply.

Of course, as always, this lie has a toehold in reality. If you are carrying on an affair with someone at the office, problems can result from that sin. Other people's sin can hurt you, too. If your business partner uses illegal means to profit, you, too, will suffer.

But let's talk about problems resulting from no sin at all. Have you ever experienced anything like that? Use the following categories to prompt your thinking.

Problems in my childhood: _____
_____
_____

Problems in my job: _____
_____
_____

Problems with my spouse: _____
_____
_____

Problems with my children: _____

_____

_____

Problems with my health: _____

_____

_____

Problems with my finances: _____

_____

_____

Do you remember how you felt during the circumstances you recorded? If you're like me, part of your pain was the frustration over not being able to answer why it happened. Sometimes there are no answers in life. Sometimes there are.

Do you recall the account in the gospel of John concerning the man born blind? The disciples quizzed Jesus about this very issue.

> His disciples asked him, "Rabbi, who sinned, this man or his parents, that he was born blind?"
>
> "Neither this man nor his parents sinned," said Jesus, "but this happened so that the work of God might be displayed in his life."
>
> John 9:2–3, NIV

In your own words, why did God allow this man to be born blind?

_____

_____

The challenge we face is to examine honestly the *root* of a given problem. If the root is a personal sin, then that sin needs to be dealt with before the personal problem can be solved.

If, on the other hand, a problem is the result of someone else's sin or no sin at all, then we need to let ourselves off the hook and solve the problem as best we can. The alternative is to spend our lives feeling guilty over something we didn't cause, all because of a lie.

IT IS MY CHRISTIAN DUTY TO MEET ALL THE NEEDS OF OTHERS

There's an old maxim in the world of group dynamics that certainly has merit. It goes like this:

Fifteen percent of the people do 85 percent of the work.

Does that saying correspond to your personal experience? If you agree with that statement, are you part of the 15 percent who do all the work, or the 85 percent who don't?

My guess is that many of you who read this workbook are in the "worker" category. (That probably was part of the motivation to buy this book in the first place!) Although there is a certain admirable quality to being so involved, it does have a downside. It could be that you are believing a lie. "It's my Christian duty to meet all the needs of others" is one way to say it. "Christians never say no" is another way to state it. Either way, it's a lie.

Have you ever been motivated to help in some way because you felt you couldn't say no? Check all the situations that apply.

- ☐ Help with your child's homework
- ☐ Teach a class at church
- ☐ Coach a child's sports team
- ☐ Buy an item for a fund-raiser
- ☐ Work the snack bar at a community event
- ☐ Sing a solo for the choir director

☐ Visit a sick person in the hospital

☐ Drive the car pool twice as much as anyone else

There is nothing wrong with any of the items on that list. At issue is not what we do but *why* we do it.

If you buy into this lie, burnout is inevitable.

When was the last time you suffered burnout? Describe the situation. *(For instance, "I volunteered to coach my son's soccer team, knowing full well I had a quarterly report due at work that demanded lots of overtime.")*

_____

_____

_____

Was your burnout related to "meeting all the needs of others" or "Christians can't say no"? Explain your answer. *(For instance, "It was clearly a case of I could not say no. I felt that if I didn't coach that team, no one would. I didn't want the guilt of the team disbanding resting on my shoulders.")*

_____

_____

_____

Many of us tend to forget a very important truth from Scripture. It is *God* who supplies needs. In reality, we only participate in that greater effort. Remember Paul's words:

I planted the seed, Apollos watered it, but God made it grow. So neither he who plants nor he who waters is anything, but only God, who makes things grow.

1 Corinthians 3:6–7, NIV

We can only do so much to meet the needs of others. God would not call us to a life of meeting others' needs in a way that burns us out in the process. A good passage to reflect on is found in Matthew's gospel:

> "Come to me, all you who are weary and burdened, and I will give you rest. Take my yoke upon you and learn from me, for I am gentle and humble in heart, and you will find rest for your souls. For my yoke is easy and my burden is light."
>
> Matthew 11:28–30, NIV

A GOOD CHRISTIAN DOESN'T FEEL ANGRY, ANXIOUS, OR DEPRESSED

Would you be surprised if I told you that many of my Christian patients feel that emotions such as anger, anxiety, and depression are wrong and automatic signs that one's faith is not up to par? You probably wouldn't be surprised, because this is a very common thought in our world today. Christians see those feelings as "negative" emotions.

The belief that we shouldn't feel what we feel often results in "stuffing." Stuffing is taking what you feel and repressing or suppressing it so that you don't feel it. The feelings don't really go away, though. They stay buried, ready to come out when we tire of expending effort to keep them stuffed. Ultimately, when too many feelings get stuffed, the result is a very messy "spewing" of the logjam of emotions—which usually happens at the most inopportune times. Playing your "A good Christian never gets angry or depressed" tape long enough can blow up in your face.

Have you had experiences that triggered great emotion? Maybe your best friend ripped you off. Or your wife left. Or your house was burglarized. Or you lost your job. Have you stuffed your anger or anxiety or depression? Have they spewed out in an inopportune moment? Write down your recollections.

My anger

The situation: _____

_____

_____

How I stuffed it: _____

_____

_____

How I spewed it: _____

_____

_____

My anxiety

The situation: _____

_____

_____

How I stuffed it: _____

_____

_____

How I spewed it: _____

_____

_____

My depression

The situation: _____

_____

_____

How I stuffed it: _____

_____

_____

How I spewed it: _____

_____

_____

I get quite a few "stuffers" in my office. They come to me because they have stuffed so long they are emotionally sick from it. It's my job to help them sort out what is taking place.

Sometimes God wants us to feel anger, anxiety, or depression. But other times, these emotions may very well indicate a lack of faith. So how does one go about determining the difference?

Let me suggest three questions to ask yourself:

1. How *often* do I feel sad (angry, anxious)?

2. How *intense* is my feeling?

3. How *long* have I experienced this feeling?

Strong emotions that show up *frequently* should make us question what is going on. Emotions that are overwhelmingly *intense* may also be a sign our faith needs tending. Finally, strong emotions that last a *long time* may signal a problem with faith.

While we need to be honest about what we feel, at the same time, we must be honest enough to examine whether or not the feeling fits what has happened to us. Neither stuffing nor spewing what we feel usually helps. The middle ground is to face what we feel, examine the validity of the emotion, and express it in ways that help others and us grow.

GOD CAN'T USE ME UNLESS I'M SPIRITUALLY STRONG

As a college student, I remember playing this tape over and over again. I would want to tell my friends about Christ, but I felt my life was such a mess that God couldn't work through me. I was convinced they'd look at my life and say, "Hey, you don't practice everything you talk about. Why should I listen to you?" Even today, I'd love to tell close friends about God, but I find myself playing that same old tape in my head. How can I tell them about God if my life doesn't show shining proof of all I'm declaring?

Can you identify with this mind-set? Actually, it's an offshoot of the self lie, "I must be perfect." How can I glorify God until I lead a perfectly perfect life? we ask.

But God, in His Word, provides the beautiful antidote to this thinking. Paul wrote this to the Christians in Corinth:

> To keep me from becoming conceited because of these surpassingly great revelations, there was given me a thorn in my flesh, a messenger of Satan, to torment me. Three times I pleaded with the Lord to take it away from me. But he said to me, "My grace is sufficient for you, for my power is made perfect in weakness." Therefore I will boast all the more gladly about my weaknesses, so that Christ's power may rest on me. That is why, for Christ's sake, I delight in weaknesses, in insults, in hardships, in persecutions, in difficulties. For when I am weak, then I am strong.
>
> 2 Corinthians 12:7–10, NIV

Can you spot two or three statements in this passage that refute this lie? Jot them down.

1. _____

2. _____

3. _____

The bottom line is that we are all "sick" and in need of the Doctor. We are always going to be less than perfect representatives of Christianity when we talk with others, no matter what level of Christian maturity we ultimately attain. Pretenses otherwise are hurtful and unhealthy. What better favor can we do potential Christians than to allow them to see the reality of the Christian struggle so they won't have misconceptions about what it is all about.

I imagine by now you're getting the idea of how these lies work and how they distort the truth. So allow me to turn the tables. Let's suppose I come to you. My problem is that I believe that God cannot use me unless I am spiritually strong, and I feel particularly weak at this time. How would you help me? Write down a strategy for me in the space that follows.

How to beat this religious lie: _____

_____

_____

_____

For those of us who believe some or all of the lies we've discussed, one of the critical actions we must take to erase our tapes is to study the Bible more carefully and see what it *really* says.

LOOKING OVER
WHERE WE'VE BEEN

Look back over the religious lies that have been presented in this chapter. I would imagine that all of us could relate to at least one of these untruths. What I would like you to do in this review is to pick the religious lie that is most damaging in your life right now. Once you have identified it, walk it through the TRUTH system. Start with a trigger event—that situation which brings out this lie in your life. It may be a situation at church, a conflict at home, or an ongoing struggle that never leaves your mind. The point is to work it through to the healthy reaction that comes from applying the truth.

Trigger Event: _____

_____

_____

_____

Reckless Thinking: _____

_____

_____

_____

Unhealthy Reaction: _____

_____

_____

_____

Truthful Thinking: _____

_____

_____

_____

Healthy Reaction: _____

_____

_____

_____

GROUP DISCUSSION STARTERS

1. How do you think religious lies get started? Isn't it somewhat of a contradiction that lies come from our religious beliefs?

How can we prevent lies from spreading further in our spiritual lives?

2. Many people understand that it is God's grace that provides salvation, but they don't understand how to live their lives by grace. Do you agree or disagree with that statement? Why or why not? Have you personally wrestled with that issue? How have you come to resolve it?

3. What does the word "forgiveness" mean to you? Why is it so difficult for some people to grasp the real meaning of forgiveness? How do you teach your children the difference between hating sin and hating the sinner in practical terms?

4. We alluded to a great debate all throughout this chapter, so let's put it out on the table: If God is a God of love, why is there so much pain and suffering in the world? How do you reconcile God's goodness with famine, flood, disease, social injustice, and the like?

5. We covered material on how our problems can stem from personal sin, someone else's sin, and no sin at all. Do you have personal experience with all three areas? Which was the most difficult to deal with? Have you believed a lie about sin in the past, and in doing so, experienced even greater pain? If comfortable, share it with the group in an encouraging way.

6. Fifteen percent of the people do 85 percent of the work. Do you agree or disagree? Would you change those figures? Why does that uneven statistic occur? Are you by nature a busy, busy, doer like Martha, or are you like Mary, who sits at the feet of her Lord?

7. Do anger, anxiety, and depression have any place in the Christian's life? Can you defend your answer with Scripture? How would you counsel a fellow Christian who is experiencing intense anger? Severe anxiety? Deep depression?

8. Do you have a personal illustration of how God has used you in a real time of weakness to minister in a very strong way? Share it with the group. Why do we as Christians tend to hide our imperfections, giving the impression that we have it all together?

9. Spend some time with your buddy in the group. Check in on his or her prayer requests—update the old ones and learn about any new ones. Also, get a brief progress report on how your buddy is doing in this study. Make sure to leave time for each of you to report to the other.

Chapter 8

THE TRUTHS WE MUST BELIEVE FOR EMOTIONAL HEALTH: PART ONE

Mature people seem to have special knowledge beyond human understanding—a "secret" to their maturity. We want to get our hands on what these people know so we can be mature, too. We spend energy, money, and time searching for their secret, whether it is the secret for getting along with others, being effective at work, or raising well-adjusted kids.

If you happen to be wondering what the secret for being an emotionally healthy person is, I believe I can tell you: It is dedication to the truth. Dedication to knowing, believing, and living the truth has always been and always will be the real cause of emotional health.

In the next two chapters of our workbook, I want to pass along to you twelve truths that I believe are among the most important for living an emotionally healthy life. These truths have been around for thousands of years, and all of us have heard them time and time again from parents, friends, coworkers, and even strangers at the checkout stand. Yet, sadly, while we have heard these truths hundreds of times before, most of us don't really believe them, much less live our lives by them. Consequently, our emotional health suffers, often greatly.

Just as exercise and proper diet are essential to physical health, these truths are essential to apply in order to have emotional health. Study them carefully. I want you to honestly examine whether or not you really believe them or live your life by them. Let's go through them one by one.

TO ERR IS HUMAN

Mistakes—more than a few of us hate to make them. Anything less than perfect just won't do. Most of us struggle with this issue all our lives. Preschoolers fight among themselves to be the first in a race. The school years come along and introduce us to report cards, that quarterly reminder of imperfection! How we would yearn for a report card that would read $A+$'s straight across the page. But so few of us ever achieved that high standard.

Then there are extracurricular activities: pressures to compete in athletics or music or drama or speech. Second place is okay, but most of us didn't go to bed every night dreaming of a silver medal—it's always been "Go for the gold."

Once we enter adulthood, it's perfection at our jobs, in our relationships with spouse, children, and friends, and a long list of other demands. What we end up with is a fanaticism for perfection. What worries me is this fanaticism makes us believe that making a mistake of any kind is horrible and proves that we are worthless as individuals. That's not only ridiculous but dangerous.

"How," you may ask, "is it dangerous?"

A person who believes that to err is stupid will make a mistake and immediately start into a self-abusive song and dance that goes something like this:

You stupid idiot! What's wrong with you? How could you have done something so imbecilic! No one else on the planet has ever done anything this ignorant. You are the only person dumb enough to have pulled this off. Great work, chump! Everyone around you must think you are the biggest moron ever born. You deserve the miserable life you're leading be-cause you are nothing but a loser from the word go. Hang your head in shame.

Do you ever feel this way? If you do, you know what accompa-nies this kind of talk—unnecessary anger, anxiety, guilt, embar-rassment, and worry. Check the emotions that most often accompany the "To err is stupid and inexcusable" lie in your life.

☐ Anger
☐ Anxiety
☐ Guilt
☐ Embarrassment
☐ Worry

On the other side of the coin, the person who believes to err is human approaches errors and failure differently. The minute he or she makes a mistake, the internal reaction is something like this:

I just messed up. I don't like it, but I did. This will take some time to correct, so I'd better get started on it. This is the same thing Linda did yesterday. Now I know how she must have felt. In fact, I see people make this sort of mistake all the time. I want to make as few mistakes as possible, so I'll try to correct what led to this mistake. This isn't the end of the world. After all, I'm only human.

Read the following statements and circle the appropriate answer.

1. Perfection is a lofty goal that cannot be achieved due to human limitations.

Agree   *Disagree*

2. While we may not be perfect, we need to strive for improvement.

Agree   *Disagree*

3. We don't need to allow our mistakes to cause us to give up prematurely.

Agree   *Disagree*

4. A person who believes that to err is stupid will make a mistake and immediately start into self-abuse.

Agree   *Disagree*

5. A person who believes that to err is human will make a mistake and will find a more realistic perspective on this matter.

Agree   *Disagree*

6. A mistake is painful enough without creating further injury with emotional self-abuse.

Agree   *Disagree*

It's important to keep in mind the truth. God makes it very clear in His Word that imperfection comes with the territory. The Old Testament says:

Surely I was sinful at birth,
    sinful from the time my mother conceived me.

                                        Psalm 51:5, NIV

It's also in the New Testament:

For in my inner being I delight in God's law; but I see another law at work in the members of my body, waging war against the law of my mind and making me a prisoner of the law of sin at work within my members.

                                        Romans 7:22–23, NIV

This is an issue of balance. Mistakes are unavoidable, but this does not give us a license to throw caution to the wind, making mistakes all over the place without concern or trying to correct them. Don't translate this issue into a lack of concern for quality. That's just as grievous a mistake as the desire to be perfect. Yes, we'll all make mistakes. But making them out of indifference or carelessness isn't healthy. As Jerry Jenkins humorously put it, "To err is human, but when the eraser wears out ahead of your pencil, you're overdoing it."

WHAT "SHOULD" HAVE HAPPENED DID

The human mind is brilliant. When a situation arises that is not to our liking, our brain has an excellent alternative that regularly goes into motion. I'm referring to the use of the word *should*. Using that word is our way of saying we don't like the reality we face. *Should* means we have a vision of a perfect world out there, and we cannot stand it when someone or something violates that world. We use this thinking on ourselves, as well as other people and situations.

Can you relate to any of these scenarios? If so, put a check mark by the appropriate ones.

- ☐ I shouldn't have said that.
- ☐ He should have been on time.
- ☐ I shouldn't have eaten so much at dinner last night.
- ☐ I should quit smoking.
- ☐ I shouldn't be so angry when I'm driving behind a slow driver.
- ☐ I should have made more time to be with my family.
- ☐ My father should have treated me better when I was younger.
- ☐ I shouldn't watch so much television.
- ☐ I shouldn't dominate the conversation so much.
- ☐ My boss shouldn't be so mean.
- ☐ I should have gone on for my master's degree.
- ☐ My mate should have told me about this issue before we married.
- ☐ I should have exercised more so I wouldn't be so unhealthy.
- ☐ Things should be different from the way they are.
- ☐ I shouldn't have gone into debt.
- ☐ I should be at church more often.
- ☐ I shouldn't have done drugs when I was younger.

Do these statements cause you to think of any others that you have used in your routine? Write them down.

_____

_____

_____

To say, "He shouldn't have been so late" actually means, "I can't accept the fact that he was so late." The reality is that if someone isn't being careful about time, how could he be anything but late? Can a person who doesn't manage his time well and waits too long before leaving get somewhere on time? In a word, no. What I am suggesting here is that it really doesn't make sense to say something like, "He shouldn't have been late," when everything the person did worked toward making sure he would be late.

Go back to the list of *shoulds* we discussed earlier. Take the one most meaningful to you, and rewrite it to reflect the true meaning of your lack of acceptance of reality. Use the blanks below:

When I said *(Fill in your "should" statement, for instance, "My boss shouldn't be so mean.")*

_____

_____.

What I really meant was *(Fill in the reality statement, for instance, "I can't accept that this is how employees are treated in a perfect world.")*

_____

_____.

Another danger that is created by this lie is that the past is never dealt with. By constantly looking back to what *should* have happened, we stay focused on what *did* happen, as opposed to what *could* happen *now* in life. It is when we focus on the present that we can begin to work on overcoming the problems created by past events.

For instance, Phil was greatly troubled by his parents' divorce. As a man of twenty-eight, he was convinced that, had that not happened fourteen years ago, he would not be as undisciplined and irresponsible as he is now. My assignment with Phil was to get him to recognize that his parent's divorce is not a situation that can be altered by saying, "It shouldn't have happened!"

The truth is, it *did* happen. Nothing can change that fact. So after Phil had some time to vent his feelings on his parents' split, I was able to direct him to some constructive action toward becoming more disciplined in his current day-to-day world.

Let's return to your *should* statement. How has this use of *should* kept your thinking focused on the past? *(For instance, "When I say 'I should have gone on for a master's degree,' I'm focusing on the past, as opposed to saying, 'What can I begin doing now to start on a master's program?'")*

_____

_____

_____

_____

_____

The next time you are tempted to say the word *should,* pause first to apply the truth of "what should have happened did" to it. If you miss an appointment because you forgot it, don't say, "I *should* have remembered." No, you forgot the appointment because you, as a human being, don't always remember everything you commit to do, and sometimes things get pushed to the back of your memory. "I should have remembered the appointment" really means, "I can't accept the fact that I forgot the appointment." Until you accept the fact that you forgot it, you won't correct whatever it was that led you to forget it.

Use the TRUTH system to identify how you have used this "should" way of false thinking. Maybe your trigger event is someone's tardiness or a long line at the grocery store or a painful event from your childhood.

Trigger Event: _____

_____

_____

_____

Reckless Thinking: _____

_____

_____

_____

Unhealthy Reaction: _____

_____

_____

_____

Truthful Thinking: _____

_____

_____

_____

Healthy Reaction: _____

_____

_____

_____

YOU CAN'T PLEASE EVERYONE

When Roger and Janice came to see me, they initially thought their problem was their marriage. But it didn't take long to determine they really loved each other, were committed to their relationship, and had no desire to get out of it. The more we talked, the more the conversation centered around Roger's work schedule. It seems he was never home, which was creating some obvious tension in Janice's life.

I asked to meet with Roger alone and, just as I suspected, certain feelings began to surface.

"What was your relationship like with your dad, Roger?" I inquired.

"Well, I wouldn't call it a relationship at all!" was Roger's initial response. I noticed as soon as I raised the issue of his father, his body language signaled discomfort.

"He was never around. He worked a lot. He grumbled a lot. It got to be where it was hard to be with him."

"Did you love him?" I asked.

"Yeah—that's what's weird about the whole thing," Roger admitted. "The truth is I never felt like I quite measured up. But I would have done anything for that man—anything."

Roger, like so many of us, has taken his deep need for approval from his father, and translated it into an obsession to please everybody else.

"Do you see the irony in this?" I asked. "In seeking something to substitute for the approval and love your father never gave you, you've been going all out for your boss, your coworkers, your customers, and everybody—everybody except Janice. And *she's* the one who wants to give you all the love and approval a man could ever want. You're treating her exactly the way your father treated you."

Roger's workaholism was jeopardizing his relationship with his wife. It also seemed to be taking a toll on his health. All of these actions go back to the need to please everyone. It just doesn't work that way.

Read the following statements and circle the appropriate response.

1. We all have a basic need for approval.

    True   *False*

2. We must have someone say something good about us in order to feel good about ourselves. Self-approval isn't good enough.

    True   *False*

3. People will be concerned about pleasing others at the expense of personal health, security of marriage, and the future of their children.

       True   *False*

4. Trying to please everyone can be as addictive as drugs and takes you to the point that you can no longer be yourself.

       True   *False*

5. All people have a basic need for intimacy.

       True   *False*

6. Pleasing God leads to finding personal satisfaction in giving. Pleasing ourselves leads to finding personal satisfaction in receiving.

       True   *False*

7. Our focus on pleasing others changes, depending on whether the action is based on pleasing self or God.

       True   *False*

8. We can please ourselves by pleasing God first.

       True   *False*

Although the truth is that we can't please everyone all the time, a lot of people keep trying anyway. If you find yourself seeking everyone's approval, don't deceive yourself into thinking it's not an addiction. It is.

Many people crave approval night and day. But the effects of approval are short-lived, so all too quickly they must seek others' approval again. It's a vicious circle, dangerous and life-threatening, but preventable.

Your focus needs to turn toward God. Pleasing God is the appropriate goal. Look at His words of comfort in John's gospel:

"The one who sent me is with me; he has not left me alone, for I always do what pleases him."

John 8:29, NIV

Jesus, our perfect example for living, found great satisfaction in pleasing His Father. You can, too.

If you consider yourself to be a person who continuously craves approval, consider developing an action plan. Take the offensive on this issue by doing the following things:

1. Admit you are enslaved to people pleasing. Don't hide it or delay facing up to it.

2. Think of all the people you have around you who will accept you *as you are*. Write down their names. *(For instance, a loving spouse, a longtime college friend or buddy from the service, neighborhood friends, church friends, extended family.)*

_____

_____

_____

_____

_____

_____

_____

3. Make an effort to cultivate some new interests that will help you meet people who will enjoy you for your company. Jot down an interest or two. *(For instance, join a community service group, or take an evening course at the local community college, or become part of the church choir.)*

_____

_____

_____

4. Create a list of priorities in your life. Write down the top five. *(For instance, Roger listed the love and care of his wife as number one. After that, he included his need for proper food, adequate sleep, enjoyable exercise, and times of recreation.)*

Priority #1: _____

Priority #2: _____

Priority #3: _____

Priority #4: _____

Priority #5: _____

5. Here's a little assignment, if you'd like to go the extra mile! Do something that purposely proves you can survive without having everyone else's approval. Do something such as:

- Yell out the time in the middle of a large store.
- Walk down the street wearing Mickey Mouse ears.
- Express a different opinion in a conversation at work.
- Say no if someone asks you to do something that you feel is an unfair request.

Write your own ideas:

_____

_____

_____

YOU DON'T HAVE TO

Margaret was relatively new to our area when she first came to see me. Her husband had been transferred to our town as a result of a promotion in his job. Margaret was proud of her husband and his accomplishment, but there was more to this story.

"I'm thrilled for Bill. This is a wonderful opportunity for him. The company is very high on him right now, and this promotion is a great career move," Margaret said in a voice that lacked excitement.

"There's more to this story, isn't there?" I suggested.

"Yes, there is," Margaret replied. "Dr. Thurman, I had to leave *my* job in order for Bill and me to make this move. Deep down I'm angry and resentful and jealous that Bill gets to move on and I have to start all over."

"Okay," I replied. "Let me ask you about something you just said. You said, 'I had to leave my job.' Let me challenge you on that, Margaret. The truth is you didn't *have* to."

"Well, of course I did!" she interrupted. "A good wife has to follow her husband. I had no choice but to quit."

"I understand what you're saying, I really do. But the truth is, Margaret, you could have chosen to stay at your job. You didn't *have* to leave. You *chose* to leave. That might sound like a small difference to you, but it's really quite an important distinction."

This was, understandably, a difficult issue for Margaret. Actually, one of the most challenging tasks we face in life is that of taking responsibility for how we feel and what we do. The natural human bent seems to be to blame other people or things for the unhappiness we feel and the actions we take. Yet blaming someone else is the ultimate cop-out.

This was the struggle underlying Margaret's resentment over the relocation. She did not want to take responsibility for the choice she had made, so she fell into a "have to" mind-set that made it easy to blame Bill for her own choice. Once she had convinced herself that she "had to" move with Bill, she built up a mountain of resentment and anger toward him, as if he were the enemy. This only added more problems to her real problem.

Do "have to" statements sound familiar to you? Check the ones you hear regularly.

☐ I have to go to work tomorrow.

☐ I have to pay my taxes.

☐ I have to obey the speed limit.

☐ I have to visit my parents.

☐ I have to finish college.

☐ I have to take my kids to the park on Saturday.

☐ I have to lose some weight.

You can probably add a few more statements that you hear often. Jot them down.

_____

_____

_____

Now let's be clear. You don't have to do anything, even though painful consequences may come your way if you choose not to do certain things. For instance, you don't have to go to work tomorrow, but you may get in trouble with your boss or possibly lose your job if you don't. You don't have to pay your taxes, but you may be in trouble with the IRS if you don't. You don't have to obey the speed limit, but you may get a ticket if you don't.

What are two or three "have to" statements that have great influence in your life? Write them down.

1. _____

2. _____

3. _____

Read the "have to" statements again, only this time, in place of *have*, substitute the word *choose*. It makes a big difference.

I choose to go to work.

I choose to stay married.

I choose to love my kids and raise them properly.

I choose to lose weight.

I choose to be happy (or unhappy) in my life.

I choose to get angry at the guy who rides my bumper.

I choose to let things from the past continue to hurt me.

I choose to allow people to treat me the way that they do.

I choose whether or not to have a satisfying life.

If these "choose to" statements ring of truth, you are on your way to living a very healthy life. If they don't, you have a lot of work to do. Keep working, though—it will be worth it.

Take the three "have to" statements you wrote down earlier, and rewrite them with the word *choose* instead.

1. _____

2. _____

3. _____

This is a good place to insert the TRUTH system. Notice how *have to* appears in the reckless thinking portion, and *choose to* appears in the truth section.

Trigger Event: _____

_____

_____

_____

Reckless Thinking: _____

_____

_____

_____

Unhealthy Reaction: _____

_____

_____

_____

Truthful Thinking: _____

_____

_____

_____

Healthy Reaction: _____

_____

_____

_____

YOU ARE GOING TO DIE

What do you want out of life? I mean what do you want out of life *specifically?* Do you know why you are working as hard as you are? Do you know what you value most? Take a minute to work the exercise that follows. Maybe this perspective would be helpful: If I had only ten more years to live, what would I rate as *essential?*

Circle the appropriate number for each statement.
    1—essential to have
    2—important to have after essentials
    3—expendable in a pinch
    4—totally frivolous

  1. Living in a nice apartment in a nice neighborhood
            1   2   3   4

2. Owning a nice home in a nice neighborhood

    1   2   3   4

3. Continuing the husband's education

    1   2   3   4

4. Continuing the wife's education

    1   2   3   4

5. Putting aside money for the children's education

    1   2   3   4

6. Buying a better car

    1   2   3   4

7. Buying a second car

    1   2   3   4

8. Owning a boat, motorcycle, camper, or RV

    1   2   3   4

9. Buying new clothes each season

    1   2   3   4

10. Buying household appliances and furnishings

    1   2   3   4

11. Remodeling the home

    1   2   3   4

12. Saving for retirement

    1   2   3   4

13. Regular saving for any purpose

      1   2   3   4

14. Eating out two or three times a week

      1   2   3   4

15. Entertaining at home on a regular basis

      1   2   3   4

16. Going to movies, the theater, or concerts regularly

      1   2   3   4

17. Travel

      1   2   3   4

18. Buying stocks or other investments

      1   2   3   4

19. Buying insurance

      1   2   3   4

20. Buying books and records regularly

      1   2   3   4

21. Having more friends

      1   2   3   4

22. Being involved in civic affairs

      1   2   3   4

23. Leading an important cause

      1   2   3   4

24. Enjoying more solitude

      1   2   3   4

25. Buying art and antiques

      1   2   3   4

26. Paying for a hobby

      1   2   3   4

27. Attending sporting events regularly

      1   2   3   4

28. Belonging to a country club or health club

      1   2   3   4

29. Contributing to charities, special causes, or political campaigns

      1   2   3   4

30. Buying expensive Christmas, birthday, and other gifts.

      1   2   3   4

Few truths have the potential to affect our lives as strongly as the one that warns, "You *are* going to *die.*" Death waits around the corner for us all. Death may be a terrible truth, but it is a truth that can be used positively to prompt us to live life more fully.

Go back and examine those thirty statements. Would you answer any of them differently with the added truth that you will die someday?

It is important for us to realize that we are going to die because it is another of God's great truths. In the book of Proverbs we read:

Do not boast about tomorrow, for you do not know what a day
may bring forth.

Proverbs 27:1, NIV

To live life to its fullest, we need to live life wisely. And to live
life wisely, we need to live it with the truth of death in a key
position in our thinking.

Draw a written "map" of your life, looking at where you've
been and where you want to go. Begin by writing a summary of
your accomplishments to date. *(For instance, high school graduate,
two years in the army, married eleven years, two great kids, church
deacon, four bowling trophies, completely rebuilt a 1965 Mustang,
became assistant manager in 1992.)*

_____

_____

_____

_____

_____

Now, write in what the date will be exactly *one year* from
today.

_____

Write down three or four things that would greatly enrich
your life if you were to accomplish them between now and one
year from now. *(For instance, reading a dozen great works of litera-
ture, attending a money management seminar, starting a sideline
business in antique jewelry, taking a class in real estate, taking piano
lessons.)*

1. _____

2. _____

3. _____
4. _____

Write in what the date will be *three years* from now.

_____

Write down three or four more accomplishments you'd like to make in your life by then.

1. _____
2. _____
3. _____
4. _____

Write in the date *ten years* from now.

_____

Write in your projected accomplishments that would enrich your life.

1. _____
2. _____
3. _____
4. _____

Write in the date *thirty years* from now.

_____

Write in your projected goals.

1. _____
2. _____
3. _____
4. _____

Next, write a *Who's Who* entry for your life that would appear at your life's end. Address your achieved goals and accomplishments.

_____

_____

_____

_____

_____

_____

Finally, what about your spiritual goals? What would you like to have accomplished spiritually one year from now?

_____

_____

Five years from now?

_____

_____

Ten years from now?

_____

_____

THE VIRTUE LIES IN THE STRUGGLE, NOT THE PRIZE

This truth has become virtually unheard of in our culture. Have you ever heard a man say he couldn't wait until retirement so that he wouldn't have to work any longer, yet once retirement came he became depressed, even suicidal, because he lost his work-related identity? The "prize" of retirement isn't all that satisfying for many if the "struggle" of the career wasn't enjoyed.

I have had my own struggles with "The virtue lies in the

struggle, not the prize" truth. My own tendency is to be so "prize-minded" that my efforts along the way get little or no credit. Graduate school was like that. I felt that contentment and "victory" were only available when I got my doctorate, not in my efforts to get it. Writing my first book, *The Lies We Believe*, was the same way. I worked hard for over a year to write it, but I didn't allow myself many feelings of accomplishment until it was completed. The effort to write it seemed to have no virtue to it, because I put my sense of victory in finishing the book.

This "scoreboard" mentality, where the effort on the field is considered less important than the final score, crushes a lot of us.

Here is a very well-known passage of Scripture from the apostle Paul:

> Brothers, I do not consider myself yet to have taken hold of it. But one thing I do: Forgetting what is behind and straining toward what is ahead, I press on toward the goal to win the prize for which God has called me heavenward in Christ Jesus.
>
> Philippians 3:13–14, NIV

Take a few minutes to paraphrase these two verses. By writing them out in your own words, you can add greater meaning and emphasis from a personal perspective.

_____

_____

_____

_____

_____

_____

The virtue lies in the struggle, not the prize. Memorize that truth. Meditate on it. Keep it available for those times you are working diligently on something and the reward is nowhere in sight. When you are fighting a weight problem and not making much progress, remind yourself the effort to lose weight is your victory. When you are fighting financial debt, remind yourself that the effort to pay off your bills is your virtue. If your marriage is faltering and all your efforts to make it better seem to be failing, remind yourself that your struggle to make the marriage better is your victory. I hope "I'm trying" can become a satisfying statement for you. More often than not, it will result in "I accomplished," which is the prize most of us want.

LOOKING OVER
WHERE WE'VE BEEN

I have challenged you to alter your traditional way of thinking about certain ideas, relationships, and concepts you've heard or experienced all your life. As a different type of review, I'd like you to write down the advantages and disadvantages of thinking the "old" way versus thinking the "new" way.

Old: To err is stupid and inexcusable
New: To err is human
   Advantages and disadvantages of the old way:

_____

_____

   Advantages and disadvantages of the new way:

_____

_____

Old: Things shouldn't be as they are
New: What should have happened did

Advantages and disadvantages of the old way:

_____

_____

_____

Advantages and disadvantages of the new way:

_____

_____

_____

Old: You can and should please everyone
New: You can't please everyone
    Advantages and disadvantages of the old way:

_____

_____

_____

    Advantages and disadvantages of the new way:

_____

_____

_____

Old: I have to
New: I choose to
    Advantages and disadvantages of the old way:

_____

_____

_____

    Advantages and disadvantages of the new way:

_____

_____

_____

Old: Death is far away/won't happen to me
New: You are going to die

Advantages and disadvantages of the old way:

_____

_____

_____

Advantages and disadvantages of the new way:

_____

_____

_____

Old: The prize is everything

New: The virtue lies in the struggle, not the prize

Advantages and disadvantages of the old way:

_____

_____

_____

Advantages and disadvantages of the new way:

_____

_____

_____

GROUP DISCUSSION STARTERS

1. Why do people hate to make mistakes? Should we try to be perfect? If mistakes are unavoidable, should we be concerned about them? What is the biblical perspective on dealing with mistakes? How can we find a balance in our approach to mistakes?

2. What are some reasons for saying, "What should have happened did"? How does the use of the word *should* reveal a person's perspective on life? Is there a personal story you can share that illustrates this truth? This can be a hard truth to grasp because it can involve situations of great pain. How can you help someone through this process?

3. How would you go about teaching your children that you can't please everyone, yet emphasizing the importance of trying to get along with and reaching out to others? Do you agree or disagree that people-pleasing can be an addiction? How does this issue tie in with a healthy self-concept?

4. Why do people so freely shirk responsibility? Why do we use "have to" instead of "choose to"? Have you ever been guilty of blaming someone else for a decision you made?

5. How has the reality of your own impending death helped you live a fuller life in the present? What is the Christian approach to life and death, based on the Bible? What would you like to have entered in your *Who's Who* entry at your death? Share with the group your approach to priorities and goals.

6. Do you know any stories of men or women who turned failure into victory, thus showing the virtue lies in the struggle, not the prize? Do you have any personal stories of this nature? What does it mean to you to "press on toward the goal to win the prize for which God has called me"?

7. Share with your buddy what's been going on in your life this week. How are the issues you two have been praying about? Are there any new requests? Be sure to allow time for both of you to share from your lives. What was the most important truth you learned in this chapter?

Chapter 9

THE TRUTHS WE MUST BELIEVE FOR EMOTIONAL HEALTH: PART TWO

Truths need to be continually examined and applied even if you have heard them thousands of times before. As A. P. Herbert put it, "Imagine how little good music there would be if, for example, a conductor refused to play Beethoven's Fifth Symphony on the ground that his audience may have heard it before." Think about how few truths we could discuss if we couldn't discuss the ones we had already heard.

The truths we are discussing are like a fine symphony. They need to be heard over and over again until you understand every little measure of what they mean. They are *that* important. My hope is that our exploring of these "old" truths is a way of making them clearer, more meaningful, and even life changing. Things that have been around for a while do have a way of losing their freshness and power. So it is with truths that have survived for centuries.

Let's continue in our discovery of what I believe to be some of the most important truths for an emotionally healthy life.

YOU ARE NOT ENTITLED

Harold was uncomfortable from the outset of our very first session. He made it clear that his discomfort level was directly related to me!

"You look to be about the same age as my son," he mused, looking me up and down. "You probably think the same way, too."

"How's that?" I asked.

"That's the problem," he began. "I was a good father. You can ask anyone about that—even Steve—he's my son. I worked hard, sometimes two jobs, so that the family had food on the table and a roof over their heads. Back then, we believed the mother should stay home, so I went through all the extra stress and strain to make the money stretch far enough to provide for us all. I helped put Steve through college and graduate school. I guess what I'm trying to say is, I was there for him, whenever and wherever."

"All right, I think I understand what you're saying," I commented. "So how does this tie in with your visit here today?"

"Well, I guess I'm disappointed in Steve," he said softly. He paused and then spoke with greater force. "No, I'm more than disappointed in Steve. I'm angry at him."

"Why?"

"Because I did all these things for him when he was growing up, taking care of him and all . . ." His voice trailed off. "And now that I need him, he's nowhere to be found."

"What do you mean?"

"My wife passed away two years ago. We were close—real close. I've been so lonely. I retired from the business about four years ago. I could use some friendship. Actually, I could use some peace of mind knowing that if I'm in a pinch, someone would be there for me."

"And that's what you're looking for with Steve."

"Exactly. But he's too busy in his own life to give me any time. Dr. Thurman, it's not right. I did all that stuff for him. He owes me. I deserve to be treated better!"

Although Harold didn't use the word, he was referring to the concept of *entitlement*. We all believe this lie to a certain extent. Our society says that we are such fantastic people that we are entitled to an equally fantastic way of living. Just listen to the advertisements that surround us:

You *deserve* a break today . . .

Pamper yourself . . .

You *owe* it to yourself . . .

You're *worth* it . . .

When we feel entitled, we focus on what we are owed, not what we might give to others. It's a "one-way street" mind-set. When these feelings are strong and people don't meet our expectations, we often become bitter, resentful, and angry, much like Harold. Relationships can be (and often are) destroyed by feelings of entitlement.

I have devised an Entitlement Quiz for you to take. For each of the fifteen statements, mark a number from one to seven to gauge your personal feeling about the statement. This vehicle will help you get a better read on the whole issue of entitlement. Use the following scale:

1	2	3	4	5	6	7
strongly disagree			neutral			strongly agree

Respond in terms of how you really feel as opposed to how you think you should feel. Do not spend too much time on any one item. Try to avoid the neutral response, if possible.

_____ I deserve respect from others.

_____ I demand good service in a restaurant.

_____ My closest friends owe me loyalty.

_____ I expect fairness from others.

_____ I'm owed a good paying job for my abilities.

_____ People should treat me the way I treat them.

_____ When I do something nice for people, I secretly expect them to do something nice for me.

_____ I deserve a "thank you" when I hold a door open for someone or let someone ahead of me in traffic.

_____ People should listen to what I have to say.

_____ I often feel "owed" for things I have done.

_____ Other people have told me I expect too much.

_____ All in all, I deserve a good life.

_____ I am entitled to "life, liberty, and the pursuit of happiness."

_____ I get angry when others don't do things for me that they said they would do.

_____ My children owe me cooperation and obedience for all the sacrifices I have made for them.

Add all the numbers of your fifteen responses; then divide that total by fifteen. The number you are left with will show you on the scale how convinced you are that you are entitled to certain things.

If your score is:

1 to 4: You really are not *expecting* much from other people in the way of gratitude, approval, and response. As such, you probably won't be disappointed in life when such responses aren't forthcoming.

5 to 7:   You are probably a person who is carrying a lot of internal anger because not enough people give you what you feel entitled to. If this is the case, you need to readjust your expectations.

Remember, you are "owed" nothing for all you do. People have the perfect freedom to fly in the face of what you want. The challenge is to do things for people because it's healthy or mature or "right," not because you can earn "green stamps" that you can cash whenever you want.

Feeling "owed" is a type of reckless thinking that leads to unhealthy reactions. Think of a common trigger event, jot it down, and work it through the TRUTH system.

Trigger Event: _____
_____
_____
_____

Reckless Thinking: _____
_____
_____
_____

Unhealthy Reaction: _____
_____
_____
_____

Truthful Thinking: _____
_____
_____
_____

Healthy Reaction: _____

_____

_____

_____

THERE IS NO GAIN WITHOUT PAIN

Our society believes that everything in life should be quick and easy. Unfortunately, this is not the case. A very important lesson in life is the understanding of "there is no gain without pain."

We all want the nice rewards of a healthy life, but we don't necessarily want to work hard to get them. The truth that personal maturity and improvement require effort and hard work is not new. It's one of those truths that's been around for a long time, but I think we need to come back to it. The desire to avoid pain and seek pleasure is something we all feel, but it runs counter to emotional health.

If you are like most folks, you have had your share of pain in your life. Before we look at the gain in your life's experiences, let's look at the trials. In the spaces that follow, write down examples of pain in each category. Don't make up answers just to fill in the blanks. But if there are genuine instances of pain in the particular category, record it.

Pain in my childhood: _____

_____

Pain in my teen years: _____

_____

Pain in college: _____

_____

Pain in my marriage: _____

_____

Pain in my parenting: _____

_____

Pain in my finances: _____

_____

Pain in my physical health: _____

_____

Pain in my emotional health: _____

_____

Pain in other areas: _____

_____

Compiling a list like this one can be painful in itself. But don't forget the truth we're examining: There is no gain without pain. Many people think this truth is contrary to the teachings of the Bible. But that is not the case. The concept of Christians suffering is woven throughout both Old and New Testaments. One of the clearest passages is found in the book of James:

> Consider it pure joy, my brothers, whenever you face trials of many kinds, because you know that the testing of your faith develops perseverance. Perseverance must finish its work so that you may be mature and complete, not lacking anything.
>
> James 1:2–4, NIV

Look at some of the key words in this passage. What do these words mean to you?

Joy: _____

Trials: _____

Many kinds: _____

Testing: _____

Faith: _____

Perseverance: _____

Mature: _____

Complete: _____

Not lacking: _____

Can you see how valuable testing can be in our lives? The pain in your life has produced great results, or else it will in the future. If you want it "easy," you have to work hard. If you want a quiz to be easy, you have to study hard. If you want a couple of hours on the tennis court to be easy, you have to train hard. If you want your marriage to be easy, you have to work diligently on making it strong. If you want life to be easy, you have to put your all into it, painfully so. There is no gain without pain. Don't let anyone tell you otherwise. If someone does, that person is lying to you.

Now let's go back over the list of painful situations you recorded earlier. This time I want you to write down the lesson you learned from each one. In other words, what is the "gain" that resulted from the "pain"?

Gain from the pain in my childhood: _____

_____

Gain from the pain in my teen years: _____

_____

Gain from the pain in my college years: _____

_____

Gain from the pain in my marriage: _____

_____

Gain from the pain in my parenting: _____

_____

Gain from the pain in my finances: _____

_____

Gain from the pain in my physical health: _____

_____

Gain from the pain in my emotional health: _____

_____

Gain from the pain in other areas: _____

_____

YOUR CHILDHOOD ISN'T OVER

A fair number of people see the past as something that is over and done. It needs to be forgotten and left behind. Yet it isn't quite that easy, is it? As much as it may seem like a self-indulgent waste of time to look backward in time, our unique personal history often demands to be examined and dealt with before life in the here and now can be lived fully.

Let me give you a thumbnail sketch of what most self-help books are saying about the importance of early childhood experiences. These books suggest that we begin life with normal needs for love, attention, and affirmation. These are all normal needs that, for a time, make us want to be the center of the universe. If these needs are adequately met, the theory goes that we can move into adulthood able to let go of the need to be the "center of attention" and able to live life as healthy, functioning adults who can give and take. If these needs are not properly met, however, the belief is that we will carry them into adulthood, with a great deal of hurt, anger, and shame attached to them, and be "dysfunctional" adults.

Furthermore, these books suggest that many of us, to some degree or another, received inadequate care from our parents and, thus, were emotionally damaged during our childhood. This damage can range from mild to severe, depending on how poorly our fathers and mothers nurtured us. The damage may have resulted from our parents' being indifferent toward us, or from their controlling us too much, or from their trying to live out their needs for attention and success through us. In extreme cases, parents damage us through sexual, verbal, physical, and/ or emotional abuse.

What do you remember about your childhood? If you were sitting in my office right now, how would you describe it to me? Jot down what comes to mind as I ask these questions:

What was your mother like? Describe her. _____

_____

_____

_____

What was the best thing about her? _____

_____

What was the worst thing about her? _____

_____

What was your father like? Describe him. _____

_____

_____

_____

What was the best thing about him? _____

_____

What was the worst thing about him? _____

_____

Did you feel accepted and loved as a child? _____
Explain your answer.

_____

_____

_____

_____

Did you feel as though you were the "center of attention" as
a child? _____ Explain your answer.

_____

_____

_____

Destructive childhood rearing leaves a child feeling unaccept-
able and believing his own feelings and uniqueness are not "okay."

A child who doesn't feel accepted will often develop a "false self" as a protective device. Do any of these false self forms sound like something you used in your childhood? Check the ones that apply.

- ☐ Pleaser
- ☐ Straight-*A* student
- ☐ Class clown
- ☐ Perfectionist
- ☐ Workaholic

Even back in Moses' time, people were aware of how critical the growing up years could be. Parents were exhorted to feed their children healthy doses of the truth at an early age. The child would not forget, and it would be an important aspect in feeling loved and affirmed.

> Fix these words of mine in your hearts and minds; tie them as symbols on your hands and bind them on your foreheads. Teach them to your children, talking about them when you sit at home and when you walk along the road, when you lie down and when you get up.
>
> Deuteronomy 11:18–19, NIV

The TRUTH system works on this issue, as well. Think of a trigger event that springs you into a painful situation from childhood. Walk through the process.

Trigger Event: _____

_____

_____

_____

Reckless Thinking: _____

_____

_____

_____

Unhealthy Reaction: _____

_____

_____

_____

Truthful Thinking: _____

_____

_____

_____

Healthy Reaction: _____

_____

_____

_____

EMOTIONAL PROBLEMS ARE GOOD

One of the most helpful inventions to the home owner has to be the smoke detector. For just a few dollars, you can install these little contraptions that will sound a deafening alarm at the first detection of smoke. In doing so, you can gather your family, move them safely outdoors away from the danger, and try to save your house from destruction. More than a few families owe a great deal of gratitude to their smoke detectors.

Human beings have their own version of a smoke detector inside themselves. Believe it or not, it is the entrance of emotional problems into our lives! That's right! It is often the painful feelings of guilt, anger, or depression that warn us that something is not quite right inside.

I realize most people don't look favorably on emotional problems, so this particular truth can be a real stretch for some.

Elizabeth was a good example. She had been coming to see me for a long time, fighting intense feelings of anger at her husband. It wasn't until she began to take her focus off her husband and put it on herself that she started to make progress.

"This isn't about all the things that John does to make you angry," I told her one day. "This is about what your anger is saying to *you*."

"Me?"

"Yes. This anger is a signal that something isn't quite right inside. You continue to get these signals, but you've chosen to ignore them. Let's start studying them, and in doing so, we'll learn a lot about you in the process."

And, sure enough, when we redirected Elizabeth's focus, we began to learn some things about her that needed to change. This produced even greater emotional strength in her life.

There are a couple of important biblical concepts to consider in this area, as well. First, it is important to understand that God does not want His people to suffer needlessly, so God wants to use bad things that happen to us for our growth and maturity. Remember Paul's words:

> And we know that in all things God works for the good of those who love him, who have been called according to his purpose.
>
> Romans 8:28, NIV

Second, it is vital to understand that pain often motivates a person to change and grow. Through this process a person gains emotional strength. Earlier in the same letter, Paul stated:

> Not only so, but we also rejoice in our sufferings, because we know that suffering produces perseverance; perseverance, character; and character, hope.
>
> Romans 5:3–4, NIV

I want you to use the truth you've just learned to initiate a self-examination exercise. The procedure is easy to follow, yet the results will be profound.

You'll notice that what follows is a heading that states Emotional Problems Are Good. Think of the specific emotional problems you are coping with now. Consider the reasons these problems are good. What are they alerting you to and making you aware of? What are the problems motivating you to do? Write down your responses. Try to come up with ten. Don't be in a hurry. Take all the time you need.

EMOTIONAL PROBLEMS ARE GOOD

1. _____
2. _____
3. _____
4. _____
5. _____
6. _____
7. _____
8. _____
9. _____
10. _____

YOU REAP WHAT YOU SOW

I have two good friends who were raised in the most opposite situations you could ever imagine. Sam was raised in midwestern rural America. A typical day for Sam always involved some sort of work with the soil. Planting, watering, fertilizing, weeding, picking crops, plowing; you name it, Sam had done it on his father's farm.

On the other extreme, Bob is a city boy. His stories of growing up have a much different ring to them. Riding subways, playing stickball in the streets, working at the corner store, sitting on the steps in front of the row houses and watching the people go by—that was Bob's world. The closest Bob ever came to farming was growing three tomato plants in his family's tiny backyard. But Bob sure was proud of those tomatoes! To hear him tell the story, when summer came and a tomato was ready to pick, it was like a national holiday! And, of course, if you believe Bob, there was never a finer tasting tomato grown anywhere in the world.

I don't know what farming experience you've had. You may be like Bob, having limited exposure to planting and picking. Or you could be like Sam, a real farmer. Or you could be somewhere in between. No matter where you are on the farming spectrum, I want you to understand a basic rule of farming that has *never* been broken. This is really deep, so hang on to your hats. Ready? Here it is:

Whatever you plant is what you're going to pick.

Let that sink in for a minute. It makes perfect sense, doesn't it? If you plant tomato seeds, you'll pick tomatoes at harvest time. If you plant corn, you'll harvest corn. It's a law of nature. Put in true farming vocabulary, you reap what you sow.

Please forgive me if I've offended your intelligence with this short treatise on farming, but there is a reason for this diatribe. The same law of nature that is at work in our fields, is at work in our lives.

Most of us live in hope that this is not true, but we can't escape it, can we? We eat a large bowl of ice cream while watching television at night, and then hope the scales won't hold us accountable the next morning. We spend money as if there were no tomorrow and hope the charge card companies will forget to bill us at the end of the month. We don't exercise, yet we expect our bodies to remain healthy and firm throughout our lives. We ignore our kids and hope they'll grow up to be mature adults.

In dozens of different ways, we act and hope that we can avoid the consequences that almost always accompany these actions.

Do you have a few favorites of this nature (eat and not get fat, speed and not get caught, spend and not have to pay)? Jot them down.

_____

_____

_____

This is not only a natural law, it is a biblical one as well. Paul stated in Galatians:

> Do not be deceived: God cannot be mocked. A man reaps what he sows. The one who sows to please his sinful nature, from that nature will reap destruction; the one who sows to please the Spirit, from the Spirit will reap eternal life.
>
> Galatians 6:7–8, NIV

People have wrestled with this truth for centuries. Part of the rub with this issue is the appearance that some people seem to get away with certain actions without consequences. You know the types of circumstances I mean. A speed demon doesn't get pulled over by the police. Someone cheats on his income tax, but the IRS doesn't audit him. A person eats everything at the table and never gains a pound.

How do you explain these "exceptions" to the rule?

_____

_____

_____

One of the greatest dangers in this law of nature involves our *thoughts*. Many of us have convinced ourselves that we don't struggle with a particular issue as long as we don't *act* on it. But, in reality, many of our current problems are the long-term reapings of unhealthy thoughts.

What is the biggest battle in your mind right now?

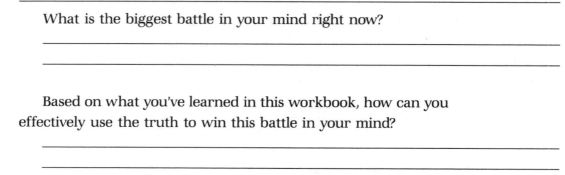

Based on what you've learned in this workbook, how can you effectively use the truth to win this battle in your mind?

Remember, while the examples of sowing and reaping in this section have focused on the negative, the flip side is equally true: Each of us can sow positive thoughts and actions and can reap the healthy consequences of doing so. The size of the healthy "seed" sown may be small, but we can choose to keep nurturing the seed until it produces truthful benefits in our lives. In this light, we also can be our own best friend.

People can sow truth in their minds over the years and reap tremendous emotional benefits. The challenge of truth, though, is to make sure it is sown properly and watered long enough to bear its reward.

LIFE IS DIFFICULT

In some ways, one central message of these chapters can be summed up in this phrase: Life is difficult. We've been working through various issues and many return to this common denominator.

I've tried to challenge you to see reality as it is in order to move toward greater levels of emotional health. Too often people seem surprised, even insulted, that life proved to be difficult, as if there were some guarantee that life would be smooth and easy. They tell their life stories with bitterness, resentment, and anger, as if life had inflicted misery solely on them.

This pain is not new. The writer of Ecclesiastes felt the same feelings back in Old Testament times.

> What does a man get for all the toil and anxious striving with which he labors under the sun? All his days his work is pain and grief; even at night his mind does not rest. This too is meaningless.
>
> Ecclesiastes 2:22–23, NIV

Life is full of difficulties. Some are necessary and some are not, but they all happen. Our choice is either to face that and accept it, or be mad at life and lose in the process.

Since we've covered so much related material already, I'm not going to beat this issue into the ground. You know how simple it is to believe the lie that life should be easy. You also know how to confront that lie with the truth. By now you are very familiar with the TRUTH system. Pinpoint a trigger event that sets off thinking in terms of life being easy or difficult. Walk yourself through the process of battling lies with the truth. Look at the clear advantage of emotional health.

Trigger Event: _____

_____

_____

_____

Reckless Thinking: _____

_____

_____

_____

Unhealthy Reaction: _____

_____

_____

_____

Truthful Thinking: _____

_____

_____

_____

Healthy Reaction: _____

_____

_____

_____

LOOKING OVER
WHERE WE'VE BEEN

In this chapter, we've looked at six more truths for living an emotionally healthy life. What follows is a list of these six truths. I'd like you to review the notes you've taken in this chapter, and then write down the most significant thing you learned about each truth. It may be something profound, or it could be something simple. The purpose of this exercise is not to impress someone with your profundity, but to recall what stands out as significant to you in your personal quest for the truth.

You Are Not Entitled

Why this is significant to me: _____

_____

_____

There Is No Gain Without Pain

Why this is significant to me: _____

_____

_____

Your Childhood Isn't Over

Why this is significant to me: _____

_____

_____

Emotional Problems Are Good

Why this is significant to me: _____

_____

_____

You Reap What You Sow

Why this is significant to me: _____

_____

_____

Life Is Difficult

Why this is significant to me: _____

_____

_____

GROUP DISCUSSION STARTERS

1. How does a person find balance between a healthy identity and the danger of feeling entitled? Share with the group what you learned from taking the entitlement quiz in this chapter.

2. Christians are notorious for advocating a life without pain—do you agree or disagree with that statement? What is a proper understanding of the biblical teaching on pain? Why do we struggle with suffering in our lives?

3. Is it difficult for you to think back on your childhood? Why or why not? Are there tangible ways you see your childhood manifesting itself in your current adult life? What are they? Do you agree or disagree with the general truth that your childhood is not over? Why?

4. How can we talk about the "good" of something "bad" like emotional problems? What is good about emotional problems, anyway? If an emotional problem is like a warning signal, why do so many of us fail to respond to the signals?

5. Why do people expect to avoid the law of sowing and reaping? Can you share a positive side of this truth? What good things have you sown in your life that have reaped positive rewards?

6. Why is it important to understand that life is difficult? What is the most important lesson you have learned about this truth as a result of this study? What have you learned about your relationship with God as a result of this study? Are you feeling more healthy emotionally? Why or why not?

7. Spend some time with your buddy. What are the prayer requests to be remembered? How is it going? What is new as a result of this study? Leave time for both of you to share.

Chapter 10

THE TRUTH ABOUT GOD

I have a friend named Gary who likes to tell me about his men's Bible study group that meets for breakfast on Wednesday mornings. On any given Wednesday, five to eight guys meet with Gary to discuss how the Bible can relate to their personal lives.

One Wednesday, Gary began the study with a question that was both simple and profound: *Who is God?*

The answers were fascinating.

"I think of God as my heavenly Father," was the first answer that came from a guy named Art. "The nice thing about God is that almost anything I ask Him to do, He'll do it."

"No, I see God very differently," Jack chimed in. "God is very just. He wants me to live a pure life." Then he added, "And if I don't live up to that standard, He'll zap me!"

"I don't think of God that way," Bart confessed. "I really see

Him as more of an old-fashioned, uncool, kind of grampa. Don't get me wrong, I believe He really loves me, but He's just a little behind the times."

Frank was next to speak. "I hate to admit this, but I've never viewed God as the kind and gentle type." He paused and stated in a whisper, "Actually, I see God as more of a mean old man whose only purpose is to keep me from having any fun in life."

Everyone had offered an opinion except Dave. Gary prompted him, "Dave, what's your view on God?"

Dave sat in silence for another few seconds and then confessed, "God is real . . . I know that . . . but He feels very far away from me right now. Sometimes I feel as if He just doesn't care about what we are doing or what is going on in our everyday lives. I wish He were closer."

As Gary retold the story to me, he made an astute observation. "All the guys had a certain degree of distortion in their beliefs about God that was negatively impacting their lives."

I wholeheartedly agreed.

I believe that an understanding of who God is is central to emotional health and spiritual maturity. It's that simple.

These five guys illustrated five very common distortions of the truth about who God is. I've given each of these distortions a name.

God Is an Indulgent Parent

This was Art's view. He saw God as someone who existed only to meet our every need and protect us from all unhappiness.

Can you identify with this distortion? Write down a situation where you believed this distortion.

_____

_____

_____

God Is a Drill Sergeant

Jack saw God as being stern. God is nothing but a rule giver who enjoys making people "drop and give me fifty" when they sin.

Do you see God this way? Record a situation where you believed this distortion.

_____

_____

_____

God Is a Nerd

This lie says God is not up on current reality. He has all these old-fashioned, unhip ways of thinking about life, liberty, and the pursuit of happiness. This was the distortion Bart bought into.

Have you bought this lie yourself? Write down a time when you believed this distortion.

_____

_____

_____

God Is a Killjoy

Frank voiced this distortion. It views God as someone who never wants us to be happy or enjoy anything.

Have you ever viewed God as a killjoy? When? Write down the circumstance.

_____

_____

_____

God Is Indifferent

Dave's distortion about God goes something like this: God exists, but He doesn't care about us, what we are doing, or what is going on in our lives.

Can you relate? Write about a situation where you felt this way about God.

_____

_____

_____

Maybe you have your own unique distortion concerning God. If so, jot it down.

_____

_____

_____

I want you to learn some undistorted truth about God. To do this, you must examine some verses from the Bible that can help you understand what God is like. Please don't think of this as a cold, impersonal study of theology. It's quite the opposite, really. J. I. Packer, in his classic book, *Knowing God*, made an important point along these lines:

> The world becomes a strange, mad, painful place, and life in it a disappointing and unpleasant business, for those who do not know God. Disregard the study of God, and you sentence yourself to stumble and blunder through life blindfolded, as it were, with no sense of direction and no understanding of what surrounds you. This way you can waste your life and lose your soul.

I have found that an understanding of the attributes of God has been a tremendous source of comfort as I face internal and external problems in my life. We have an awesome God. Let's look at some of His attributes.

GOD IS SELF-EXISTENT

Have you ever stopped to consider the fact that God has no beginning? He wasn't created—He has always existed. This prayer of Moses was recorded in the book of Psalms:

> Before the mountains were born
> or you brought forth the earth and the world,
> from everlasting to everlasting you are God.
>
> Psalm 90:2, NIV

What does the phrase "everlasting to everlasting" mean?

_____

_____

Why do you think it's important to understand that God is self-existent?

_____

_____

How does God's self-existence make a difference in the way you view Him?

_____

_____

John begins his gospel account by emphasizing that Jesus (the Word) was with God and was God from the beginning. He wrote:

In the beginning was the Word, and the Word was with God, and the Word was God. He was in the beginning with God. All

things were made through Him, and without Him nothing was
made that was made. In Him was life, and the life was the light
of men. And the light shines in the darkness, and the darkness
did not comprehend it.

John 1:1–5

I think it's very important to understand that we are God's
creation, but nothing created Him.

GOD IS OMNIPOTENT

David described God's awesome power in these terms:

> Great is the LORD, and greatly to be praised;
> And His greatness is unsearchable.   Psalm 145:3

God has complete and total power over His creation. Think
about it.

What is outside God's control?

_____

Read Luke 1:37. Is anything impossible for God?

_____

What can disrupt God's plan?

_____

What does this doctrine of God's omnipotence (having all
power) mean to you?

_____

_____

GOD IS OMNIPRESENT

Have you ever felt that God was too busy for you? Sometimes we conjure up the mental picture of a long line of people, each waiting his or her turn to have a moment to speak with God.

But that's not the way it is. God is everywhere. Theologians call that His omnipresence. You don't have to wait for Him to finish with someone before He can turn his attention to you. David wrote:

> Where can I go from Your Spirit?
> Or where can I flee from Your presence?
> If I ascend into heaven, You are there;
> If I make my bed in hell, behold, You are there.
> If I take the wings of the morning,
> And dwell in the uttermost parts of the sea,
> Even there Your hand shall lead me,
> And Your right hand shall hold me.
> Psalm 139:7–10

What is David's personal reflection concerning God's omnipresence?

_____

_____

Have you ever felt like there was no place to hide from God? Describe how it felt.

_____

_____

What encouragement is there in God being everywhere?

_____

_____

GOD IS OMNISCIENT

God knows everything.

> Great is our Lord, and mighty in power;
> His understanding is infinite.
>
> Psalm 147:5

Omniscience means all-knowing. God knows so much more than we do, it isn't even fair to attempt to compare. Paul wrote:

> Oh, the depth of the riches both of the wisdom and
>   knowledge of God!
> How unsearchable are His judgments and His ways
>   past finding out!
>
> "For who has known the mind of the Lord?
> Or who has become His counselor?"
> "Or who has first given to Him
> And it shall be repaid to him?"
>
> For of Him and through Him and to Him are all
>   things, to whom be glory forever. Amen.
>
> Romans 11:33–36

Look at the beauty of those terms! What do some of those phrases mean to you?

Depth of the riches: _____

_____

Wisdom and knowledge: _____

_____

Unsearchable: _____

_____

Ways past finding out: _____

_____

What does all this mean to you in your personal life? What difference does it make to you that God knows everything?

_____

_____

_____

GOD IS HOLY

One of the lessons human beings learn in life is: People will let you down. Whether it's a moral failure, an untruth, or an unkept promise, even our best friends disappoint us occasionally.

But the wonderful contrast to humans is God. He is holy. He does not disappoint.

> No one is holy like the LORD,
> For there is none besides You,
> Nor is there any rock like our God.
>
> 1 Samuel 2:2

God is distinct from anything else, completely pure and righteous. He only does what is right.

How does God's holiness affect the standards you have in your life?

_____

_____

What does it really mean to you to be holy?

_____

_____

GOD IS GOOD

This attribute is one of my favorites because of its sheer simplicity. Among all the glowing terms used to describe God's character, it's nice to know He's just plain good.

> Good and upright is the LORD;
> Therefore He teaches sinners in the way.
>
> Psalm 25:8

Everything God does is good. I find that incredibly encouraging. God can take anything that happens to us and ultimately bring good out of it. Remember Romans 8:28?

> And we know that in all things God works for the good of those who love him, who have been called according to his purpose.
>
> Romans 8:28, NIV

In your own words, write why you think it's important to understand that God is good.

_____

_____

_____

GOD IS JUST

If you're like me, you get bothered when people get away with stuff without punishment. Here, however, is an attribute of God that refutes that thinking.

> "Far be it from You to do such a thing as this, to slay the righteous with the wicked, so that the righteous should be as the wicked; far be it from You! Shall not the Judge of all the earth do right?"
>
> Genesis 18:25

God is just. He is going to do what is right. People will get their due. The guilty will be punished and the righteous will be rewarded.

What does the word *just* mean to you?

_____

_____

_____

_____

How does God's justice affect the way you live your life?

_____

_____

_____

_____

GOD IS MERCIFUL

One of the most endearing qualities of God is His mercy. I am grateful that sometimes He gives less punishment to wrongdoers than they deserve and more reward to "right doers" than they deserve. Paul wrote of this truth in Romans:

For he says to Moses,

"I will have mercy on whom I have mercy,
and I will have compassion on whom I have compassion."

Romans 9:15, NIV

What's a good definition of *mercy?* Check a dictionary or, better yet, a Bible dictionary.

_____

_____

Peter wrote of God's mercy in his first letter:

Blessed be the God and Father of our Lord Jesus Christ, who according to His abundant mercy has begotten us again to a living hope through the resurrection of Jesus Christ from the dead.

1 Peter 1:3

According to this verse, how does God demonstrate His mercy to us as humans?

_____

Can you think of other ways that God demonstrates mercy to us in a general sense?

_____

_____

Are there specific instances in your life where you received God's mercy? Jot them down.

_____

_____

GOD IS SOVEREIGN

One of the most frustrating aspects of relationships is when people let you down. Oftentimes, the situation was totally out of their control, but nonetheless, they disappointed you.

Our relationship with God is different than that. As a matter of fact, it's just the opposite. Nothing gets by God—nothing is out of His control. The fact that He controls the universe is called *sovereignty*. It's the same term one uses to describe a king over his dominion.

In Psalms it says:

Whatever the LORD pleases He does,
In heaven and in earth,
In the seas and in all deep places.

Psalm 135:6

Part of God's control over the universe involves you. In His sovereignty, God has a plan for your life. Based on what you know of God, write down some aspects of that plan. Be as specific as possible.

_____
_____
_____
_____

Now go back over that plan and ask yourself, "How am I doing in fulfilling that plan?" Are you making progress or spinning your wheels? How would you describe your progress in His plan?

_____
_____
_____
_____

Many times we want to take away this attribute from God. *We* want the control. *We* want to run our lives, at least until we botch it! Why do you think people want this control, when they know God's plan is better?

_____
_____
_____

What have you learned about God's sovereignty that can make a difference in your life?

_____

_____

_____

GOD IS UNCHANGING

Have you ever attended one of your high school reunions? Isn't it an eye-opening experience? It's rather humorous to go back after ten, fifteen, or twenty years to see how people have changed. It's rather shocking to see the star athlete at middle age carrying a few extra pounds around his midsection. And, of course, who could have known back then that the quiet little guy in the back of the room would become the chief executive officer of a multinational corporation! People do change!

But God stays the same. He doesn't change. Theologians call this His *immutability*. God is the same all the time in that He is never inconsistent or growing/developing. He is the same God from one day to another in terms of His character traits. In the Old Testament it states:

> "For I am the LORD, I do not change;
> Therefore you are not consumed, O sons of Jacob."
>
> Malachi 3:6

In the New Testament, James wrote about God's immutability:

> Every good and perfect gift is from above, coming down from the Father of the heavenly lights, who does not change like shifting shadows.
>
> James 1:17, NIV

Our God is described here as the one "who does not change." So many of the terms in this verse hold great meaning for us. What do these words or phrases mean to you?

good and perfect gift: _____

_____

Father of the heavenly lights: _____

_____

shifting shadows: _____

_____

Since God doesn't change, what does that mean to you and your relationship with Him?

_____

_____

_____

GOD IS LOVE

I saved the best for last. God loves us. Everything He does is for our best and is completely unselfish. Because of His love, He is greatly concerned about us and acts to help us. John wrote:

Whoever does not love does not know God, because God is love.

1 John 4:8, NIV

No matter if you've never felt loved on the human level by Mom or Dad or husband or wife, God loves you. You can count on it. And His love is constant. It's not related to our actions. You don't have to earn it or win it. His love is there for you all the time.

It is His love that opens the door to a relationship with Him.

But God, who is rich in mercy, because of His great love with which He loved us, even when we were dead in trespasses, made us alive together with Christ (by grace you have been saved), and raised us up together, and made us sit together in the heavenly places in Christ Jesus, . . . For by grace you have been saved through faith, and that not of yourselves; it is the gift of God, not of works, lest anyone should boast.

Ephesians 2:4–6, 8–9

I can find at least four different characteristics of God described in this passage. Look for them and list them.

1. _____
_____

2. _____
_____

3. _____
_____

4. _____
_____

I can also find five ways God has demonstrated His love to us. Find them and list them.

1. _____
_____

2. _____
_____

3. _____
_____

4. _____

_____

5. _____

_____

Because God loves us, He will demonstrate His love in various ways. The writer of Hebrews stated another demonstration:

> "For whom the LORD loves He chastens,
> And scourges every son whom He receives."
>
> Hebrews 12:6

According to this verse, how does God demonstrate His love to us?

_____

_____

Have you ever experienced God's discipline? What was the circumstance?

_____

_____

What is the most meaningful aspect of God's love for you in your life?

_____

_____

LOOKING OVER
WHERE WE'VE BEEN

I have presented these attributes of God's character to assist you in seeing the truth about God. Distortions about God cause real damage to our emotional health and our spiritual life. It's important to see who God is, and how that relates to us as individuals. As a review, I'd like you to go back over the qualities we discussed and summarize what you've learned. To help you, I've restated each attribute, leaving space for you to write in your own words what it says about God. Also, I've provided space for you to write what it means in your life, as well.

God Is Self-Existent

What that says about God: _____

_____

_____

What that means to me: _____

_____

_____

God Is Omnipotent

What that says about God: _____

_____

_____

What that means to me: _____

_____

_____

God Is Omnipresent

What that says about God: _____

_____

_____

What that means to me: _____

_____

_____

God Is Omniscient

What that says about God: _____

_____

_____

What that means to me: _____

_____

_____

God Is Holy

What that says about God: _____

_____

_____

What that means to me: _____

_____

_____

God Is Good

What that says about God: _____

_____

_____

What that means to me: _____

_____

_____

God Is Just

What that says about God: _____

_____

_____

What that means to me: _____

_____

_____

God Is Merciful

What that says about God: _____

_____

_____

What that means to me: _____

_____

_____

God Is Sovereign

What that says about God: _____

_____

_____

What that means to me: _____

_____

_____

God Is Unchanging

What that says about God: _____

_____

_____

What that means to me: _____

_____

_____

God Is Love

What that says about God: _____

_____

_____

What that means to me: _____

_____

_____

GROUP DISCUSSION STARTERS

1. Why is it important to understand that God is self-existent? Did you grow up believing this truth, or did you believe a distortion? Share your experience with the group.

2. Have you ever felt that God wasn't all-powerful? Did you ever feel like there were situations that appeared out of even *His* control? Did this situation ever rectify itself?

3. Could you relate to the Psalms that spoke of not being able to hide from God? Have you wanted to hide from God? What was the circumstance?

4. What does it mean to you to know that God is *holy?* Is that helpful or is it intimidating? How have you come to develop a proper understanding of God's holiness? How would you teach it to someone else?

5. Share what you believe is the most vivid illustration of the truth of Romans 8:28. How did this demonstrate God's goodness?

6. How can God's justice and God's mercy coexist? Don't they contradict each other? Do they cancel each other out? Do you understand how these two very different qualities of God fit together?

7. If everything is under God's control (sovereignty), what about a person's free will to make his or her own choices?

8. What is the most comforting aspect of God's character to you? Many people point to His *unchanging* nature. Have you had a personal experience with God's immutability? Why is it a comfort to know that He is unchangeable?

9. What's the best story of God's love you've heard? What's the best experience you've had of God's love? How would you communicate God's love to someone who had never heard of God or experienced His love? Have you ever been disciplined by God? At the time, did you see it as an act of love? How does God's love help you in your relationship with your spouse? Your children? Your friends?

10. Go around the room and have each person state the attribute of God that means the most to him/her. Include the reason why. It may be that you've always felt this way, or it could be a result of something you learned in this study.

11. Spend some time with your buddy, catching up on prayer requests and what's new in his or her life. How did this chapter affect you two? Did you gain any significant insights as a result of the study? Be sure to allow time for both of you to share.

Chapter 11

THE TRUTH ABOUT YOU

Patty was an attractive woman in her late thirties. On the outside, she appeared to have it all together. She was a smart dresser, gave off an air of confidence, was friendly and helpful to others. But deep down inside Patty was very different than her outward appearance. She was full of self-doubt and insecurity.

"I'm sure it goes back to my childhood," she started. "I was overweight, and kids made fun of me without mercy."

"What sorts of memories do you have of growing up?" I asked.

"Bad memories—painful ones," she recalled. "I remember being called 'Fatty Patty' by the kids. I remember when they chose sides for playground games, I was always last to be picked. I can still see myself asking to be chosen, totally humiliating myself, just to be picked."

"Were your parents supportive of you at this time?" I inquired.

"Yes and no," Patty responded. "I know Mom and Dad loved

me, but they tended to downplay what I was going through. I don't think they really understood the pain I was experiencing." She laughed and added, "I can still recall my mom telling me that everything would be all right. Then she would bring me a big piece of pie and say, 'Here, eat this pie, it'll help make things better.'" Patty began to softly sob into a tissue.

"It sounds to me like one of the only ways your mom knew how to express her love was to give you lots of food," I suggested.

"That's exactly what it was, Dr. Thurman. She said 'I love you' by giving me desserts. She would say how she never had dessert growing up during the Depression. She was so proud that she could do that for me. And, of course, I would eat every bite."

"Please go on with your story," I gently prodded.

"Well, the main issue is that I still feel the same way today as I did back then. When I went off to college, I lost a lot of weight and began to take real pride in my appearance. I've been real disciplined in my diet and exercise. A lot of good things have happened to me in my adult life. But I'm still the little fat girl deep down inside. I feel like I don't have anything to offer."

"Do you really believe that?"

She paused. "Yes, I'm afraid I really do. I just feel like a big zero—a loser."

I couldn't begin to estimate how many people I've spoken with who have a story similar to Patty's. Some details change: Some people think they are too thin or too short or their teeth stick out too far. Some had nonsupportive parents who constantly told them, "You're a stupid idiot" and "You'll never amount to anything." Some people have totally changed their physical appearance in adulthood; others have attempted to resolve their insecurities through achievement, and these lies are crushing them as adults. The details vary, but the bottom line message is still the same. Somewhere along the line they were led to believe certain lies about themselves. In this chapter I want to clear up some of those distortions. I want you to see the truth about you. More specifically, I want you to see yourself as God sees you.

I believe that the Bible is very clear on what happens to a person when he or she enters into a relationship with God. When you accepted Jesus Christ as your personal Savior, a whole new world of identity was opened up to you. I know a lot of Christians who have no idea who they are and all that they have in Christ. Since they are unaware of those truths, they are prime candidates for the inaccurate self-images that cause tremendous damage. Since you have trusted in Christ, look at the following promises the Scriptures declare.

YOU ARE A SPECIAL CREATION OF GOD

One of the most encouraging passages in the Bible is found in Psalm 139. Here King David stated some important truths:

> For you created my inmost being;
>> you knit me together in my mother's womb.
> I praise you because I am fearfully and
>>> wonderfully made;
>> your works are wonderful,
>> I know that full well.
> My frame was not hidden from you when I was made in
>> the secret place.
> When I was woven together in the depths of the earth,
>> your eyes saw my unformed body.
> All the days ordained for me
>> were written in your book
>> before one of them came to be.
>
> Psalm 139:13–16, NIV

What does it mean to you personally to be "knit together" by God?

_____

_____

What does it mean to you personally to be "fearfully and wonderfully made"?

_____

_____

I believe this passage teaches us that God created your unique features even before you were born. Examine your physical uniqueness now. What are your unique physical characteristics? *(For instance, tall build, blue eyes, long fingers.)*

_____

_____

_____

_____

Now, based on what you just listed, write a positive statement about your uniqueness.

_____

_____

YOU ARE OF INFINITE VALUE TO GOD

I want to ask you a question that isn't easy to answer. It will require some thought, but I want you to be as honest as possible. What do you think you're worth? Don't answer in dollar and cents terms, but in broader terms.

_____

_____

_____

The value of an object is often reflected by the price we are willing to pay for it. Have you ever considered what God was willing to "pay" for you? Look at Paul's words:

For there is one God and one mediator between God and men, the man Christ Jesus, who gave himself as a ransom for all men—the testimony given in its proper time.

1 Timothy 2:5–6, NIV

What was God willing to pay for you?

_____

_____

What are you worth to God?

_____

_____

How does what you are worth to God compare to what you felt you were worth in the beginning of this section? (Circle one.)

Alike   *Similar*   *Different*

If you're like a lot of people, your own view is different from God's view. That's why this section is so important. Use this portion of your study to ask God for His help. Ask Him to help you see your value from His perspective. An important question to ask over and over is:

How can I belittle myself if God has placed
such a high value on me?

YOU HAVE BEEN ADOPTED BY GOD

Have you ever been at a party where people play games that are made up of fantasy questions? They'll ask questions such as,

"If you could be any person in history, who would you be?" or "If you were a type of car, what kind of car would you be?" Well here's one I want you to answer:

If you could choose any person from history to be your father, who would you choose?

_____

Do you think he would choose you? Why or why not?

_____

_____

_____

I have no idea who you chose as your fantasy father. It may have been that you chose a king or a president or a movie star or a sports hero or a minister. But let's leave fantasyland and look at the truth. Besides your earthly father, there is another Father who has willingly adopted you. Paul wrote about this in his letter to the Ephesians:

In love he predestined us to be adopted as his sons through Jesus Christ, in accordance with his pleasure and will—to the praise of his glorious grace, which he has freely given us in the One he loves.

Ephesians 1:4–6, NIV

The passage states God adopted us "in accordance with his pleasure and will." What does this mean to you?

_____

_____

What is inconsistent about the following statement?

I know God has adopted me, but I just can't stand myself!

YOU ARE A CHILD OF GOD

Our parents have provided us with some sense of identity. When you ask the question, "Who am I?" part of your answer will reflect where you've come from. Think about it. What sense of identity have you gained from your parents? *(For instance, "I'm part German and part English, and I've been brought up Baptist.")*

Now think of this hypothetical situation: If the president of the United States were your father, how would this affect your identity?

If your father were president of the United States, you'd be pretty well taken care of, wouldn't you? If you're like most folks, that would be a pretty satisfying feeling. But actually, there is a truth that far outshines having the president for your father. God is your Father! You are His child! One of Jesus' disciples, John, wrote about this great truth:

> How great is the love the Father has lavished on us, that we should be called children of God! And that is what we are! The reason the world does not know us is that it did not know him.
>
> 1 John 3:1, NIV

Why did God call us His "children"? It's because He "lavished" us with His "great" _____.

What does the word *lavish* mean to you?

_____

_____

For many of us, being called a child of God is almost trite. Try to think of this truth like you've never thought of it before. What does it mean to you to be called God's child?

_____

_____

_____

YOU ARE A BROTHER OR SISTER TO JESUS

Many times people who are down on themselves walk around carrying a lot of shame. They dwell on bad things they've done or bad things that happened to them. This issue of shame becomes particularly potent when we think of our relationship to God. We convince ourselves that God is so upset at us over what we've done that He is actually ashamed of us! Read the words of the writer to the Hebrews:

> Both the one who makes men holy and those who are
> made holy are of the same family. So Jesus is not
> ashamed to call them brothers. He says,
> "I will declare your name to my brothers;
> in the presence of the congregation I will sing your
> praises."
> Hebrews 2:11–12, NIV

That's a passage loaded with powerful truth! Take a few minutes to paraphrase that text.

_____

_____

_____

What does Jesus call you in this passage?

_____

What does that mean to you?

_____

_____

What does this passage say about the issue of being ashamed?

_____

_____

What does it mean to you to be the brother or sister of Jesus?

_____

_____

YOU ARE A JOINT HEIR WITH CHRIST

Have you ever been jealous of someone who appeared to have it all? You know the kind of person I'm talking about. He wears all the right clothes, drives the right car, lives in the right neighborhood, eats at the right restaurants, hangs out with all the right people. I remember seeing someone like this and later finding out that this person had inherited all his money and power. Just think of it. All he did to have it all was to be born into the right family, and then he simply inherited it!

That's what it means to be an heir. You inherit what is legally or naturally a part of your parents' estate. Think of the spiritual implications of this concept. With God as your Father, you inherit from Him. Paul wrote of this in his letter to the Galatians:

> Because you are sons, God sent the Spirit of his Son into our hearts, the Spirit who calls out, "Abba, father." So you are no longer a slave, but a son; and since you are a son, God has made you also an heir.
>
> Galatians 4:6–7, NIV

Look at the key words of this passage. The word *Abba* is difficult to translate from the original text, but the closest expression we have today in our culture is *Daddy*. What does it mean to you to be allowed to call the God of the universe "Daddy"?

_____

_____

Can you think of three things off the top of your head that are part of your inheritance? *(For instance, "I have certain gifts or talents God has given me," or "I have God's protection and help in times of trouble.")*

1. _____
2. _____
3. _____

Not only are you an heir, but you are a joint heir. That means you share in this inheritance. The amazing part of this truth is that you are a co-heir with Jesus Christ! Think about that for a few minutes.

How does being a co-heir with Jesus Christ offer a contrast to feelings of self-hate and self-rejection?

_____

_____

YOU HAVE THE HOLY SPIRIT AS A GUARANTEE OF YOUR INHERITANCE

In the beginning of this chapter, I recounted to you the story of Patty. As she was growing up, she felt insecure because of her weight problem. Her playmates made fun of her, and that ridicule left some pretty serious scars on her emotions.

Patty told me one day how this affected her personal life, even today as an adult. "I still have this horrible feeling that nobody likes me. I hate to be as alone as I am, but I honestly believe that no one wants to be around me."

"Why do you feel no one cares to be with you?" I asked.

"Well, because I'm such a loser," she responded. "It would be embarrassing for someone to be seen with me." She paused. "You know it's important in our day and age to only hang around with people who make you look good!"

Although I didn't agree with her reasoning or logic, I could certainly understand her hurt.

"Patty, what if I were to tell you that there is someone who 'hangs out with you' who would make you feel very special. Would that encourage you?"

"Sure."

"Okay. Listen to this. Because you are a Christian, God has given you a wonderful gift. God has given you the Holy Spirit as a personal companion. Do you understand what I am saying? God's Spirit lives inside you. He is there *always*, as a loyal friend. He will listen to you when no one else will. I really believe that other people would enjoy being around you, Patty. But I can guarantee you that the Holy Spirit is always there for you."

Isn't that a comforting truth? If you are a Christian, the Holy Spirit is there. Guaranteed. The key passage is in Ephesians:

And you also were included in Christ when you heard the word of truth, the gospel of your salvation. Having believed, you were marked in him with a seal, the promised Holy Spirit, who is a deposit guaranteeing our inheritance until the redemption of those who are God's possession—to the praise of his glory.

Ephesians 1:13–14, NIV

We hear a lot about guarantees in commercials and advertisements. It's the sponsor's way of saying he stands behind his product. Isn't it great that God stands behind our salvation by giving us the Holy Spirit as His guarantee?

Do you have a personal understanding of the Holy Spirit living inside you? Can you describe what it means to you to have God's Spirit always with you?

_____

_____

_____

_____

This passage states that the Holy Spirit is our guarantee—"to the praise of his glory." How does the Holy Spirit in your life give glory to God? Be as specific and practical as you can. *(For instance, "Because of the Spirit in my life, I can live a holy life—without Him I couldn't.")*

_____

_____

_____

_____

To many Christians, the Holy Spirit living within them is nothing more than a doctrinal truth without practical application. If this is the case in your life, I'd like you to spend a few minutes praying—right now. I'd like you to ask God to help you appreciate the guarantee of your inheritance. State to God your desire to have the Holy Spirit become more real to you, and ask Him for His help in making that a reality in your life.

YOU HAVE JESUS' LIFE WITHIN YOU

Patty began making exceptional progress in her view of herself. There were many spiritual truths that were helpful to her in this process. It was fascinating for me to watch this person journey down such an exciting path!

Part of the help Patty received was in dealing with another distortion we create in our lives. She said to me one day in a session:

"I just can't change the way I think. I don't have what it takes to develop new thinking."

"But you can, Patty," I quickly responded. It was at this point that I gave her the assignment of reading an important passage in Paul's letter to the Colossians. It states:

Set your minds on things above, not on earthly things. For you died, and your life is now hidden with Christ in God. When Christ, who is your life, appears, then you also will appear with him in glory.

Colossians 3:2–4, NIV

We discussed this passage briefly in chapter 1, but it deserves a more detailed examination. Begin by writing this passage in your own words to give further depth and meaning to each of the key phrases in this text.

_____

_____

_____

What does this passage suggest about your thinking? Where do you place your thoughts?

_____

_____

With Christ in you, is it possible to change your thinking? Why or why not?

_____

_____

How does this passage contrast with feelings of defeat, doubt, and weakness?

_____

_____

As Jesus lives in you, He will change you. You aren't hopelessly bound to your past or your weaknesses. Ask God to help you believe that Jesus lives in you and that you can change. Thank Him that Jesus not only shows us how to live, but by living within us, He enables us to live like Him. In that sense, we imitate Him.

YOU HAVE JESUS' RIGHTEOUSNESS

Part of seeing yourself in an emotionally healthy way is seeing yourself realistically. Too many of us tend to dwell on the short-comings in our lives. This sort of negative thinking is damaging and defeating.

The key to a proper understanding of self is to see ourselves as God sees us. This is a major point in the Bible. In a sense, it was what Jesus' visit to earth was all about. Paul wrote:

> God made him who had no sin to be sin for us, so that in him we might become the righteousness of God.
>
> 2 Corinthians 5:21, NIV

When Jesus, as your substitute, took your sin, you received His perfect righteousness. This is the core of the Bible's teaching—your acceptance by God is because of Jesus, not because of your performance.

Have you tried to gain people's acceptance and approval by doing things? I think probably all of us have tried this to a certain degree. What sorts of things do you try to do?

_____

_____

Do you try to do things in order to feel accepted by God? If so, what sorts of things do you do?

_____

_____

What does this passage teach us about our relationship to God?

_____

_____

What can you learn about yourself from this verse? How does God really see you?

_____

_____

YOU WILL NEVER BE CONDEMNED BY GOD

Patty shared with me how she would self-destruct in her relationships.

"I would occasionally be asked out on a date," she began. "But I would usually decline or just go out once."

"Why was that?" I asked.

"Basically because I can't stand rejection," she replied. "I've always felt that if someone asked me out, he must not really know me. So in order to avoid the rejection I knew was ahead, I turned *him* down, before he could do it to me. It worked pretty well."

Rejection is one of the most painful experiences we'll ever encounter. Some of us transfer our feelings of rejection onto *all* our relationships—including our relationship to God. However, we need not feel rejection from God. Paul stated in clear terms to the Romans:

> Therefore, there is now no condemnation for those who are in Christ Jesus, because through Christ Jesus the law of the Spirit of life set me free from the law of sin and death.
>
> Romans 8:1–2, NIV

What does the word *condemnation* mean in this passage?

_____

What does it mean to be set free from the law of sin and death?

_____

_____

What is being taught about rejection in this text?

_____

_____

According to this passage, if I see myself as God sees me, what do I see?

_____

_____

YOU ARE A FOREIGNER IN THIS WORLD

Earlier in this workbook we talked about the need some of us have to be loved and accepted by *everybody*. Keeping everyone happy is quite an unrealistic expectation and an unnecessary pressure to put on ourselves. Read this important truth:

Dear friends, I urge you, as aliens and strangers in the world, to abstain from sinful desires, which war against your soul.

1 Peter 2:11, NIV

Once, as part of the world, you were a stranger and foreigner to God. Now, as a Christian, what is your new status, based on this verse?

_____

_____

What does it mean to you to be an alien and stranger in this world?

_____

_____

What does this text teach about gaining everyone's love and approval?

_____

_____

Because you are a Christian, you are now a "displaced person" or a "migrant" in this world. However, that's because your citizenship is in heaven! Because you are in God's family, you will live under different values and priorities. As a result, you will be misunderstood by those who are not Christians. Have you been misunderstood recently? What happened?

_____

_____

How does this verse help you defeat the lie that you can please everyone?

_____

_____

YOU HAVE UNIQUE GOD-GIVEN ABILITIES

You have a very special role in the family of God. God has equipped you with certain gifts that enable you to fulfill your special role. While no individual has all of God's spiritual endowment, your gifts have been especially designed by God to benefit the whole family.

> Just as each of us has one body with many members, and these members do not all have the same function, so in Christ we who are many form one body, and each member belongs to all the others. We have different gifts, according to the grace given us.
>
> Romans 12:4–6a, NIV

No member of God's family is useless or unnecessary. You were made by God to make a valuable contribution to the body of Christ. Do you know what it is? Can you state it in specific terms?

_____

_____

_____

The Holy Spirit has gifted you. You have certain talents that are from Him for a specific purpose. Write down as many as five abilities that you possess.

_____

1. _____
2. _____
3. _____
4. _____
5. _____

Can you state reasons why you think God gave you these abilities?

1. _____
2. _____
3. _____
4. _____
5. _____

Take a moment to thank God that He has gifted you. Ask Him to continue to help you find your "place" in His body. Remember, God doesn't make exact duplicates, so ask Him to help you to stop comparing your giftedness to others.

YOU HAVE A CHALLENGING VOCATION

Have you ever visited Washington, D.C.? It's quite an experience to view our government in action. I think part of the package is to feel the pride in observing the pomp and pageantry that so often occurs in governmental events. Whether it's a military parade, a long limousine with tiny American flags waving on the hood, or a stirring version of the National Anthem, it feels great to be an American. This is intensified if you've ever been out of the country and seen the U.S. embassy in that given land.

If you're reading this right now in your house or apartment, do you realize you are in an embassy? That's right—for you, as a Christian, are an ambassador. Paul told the Corinthians:

We are therefore Christ's ambassadors, as though God were making his appeal through us. We implore you on Christ's behalf: Be reconciled to God.

2 Corinthians 5:20, NIV

You do have a challenging vocation. You represent Christ as His ambassador to the world. What words or phrases come to mind when you think of an ambassador?

_____

_____

List some qualities you feel a good ambassador must possess.

_____

_____

As ambassador, what is the message you are to communicate, according to this passage?

_____

_____

How does being an ambassador counteract feelings of unimportance or meaninglessness in your life?

_____

_____

YOU CAN CONFIDENTLY ASK GOD FOR HELP

If you're the kind of person who tends to be down on himself, you probably feel like you're a burden on people as well. "I don't want to trouble them with my struggles," is a phrase you've used on occasion.

These feelings of inferiority can surface in our spiritual life, as well. We may find ourselves saying, "I don't want to bother

God with my problems." But the truth is, God desires to hear from us—about everything.

> Let us then approach the throne of grace with confidence, so that we may receive mercy and find grace to help us in our time of need.
>
> Hebrews 4:16, NIV

What do these words mean to you?

Approach: _____

_____

Throne of grace: _____

_____

Confidence: _____

_____

Mercy: _____

_____

Grace: _____

_____

Help: _____

_____

Time of need: _____

_____

God's throne is not a throne of doom or terror but of grace. Jesus sits on the right hand of this throne, and our relationship to Him can give us inspiration and confidence. We can talk to the Father, not as a stranger, but as part of the royal family.

Notice, also, that this help isn't conditional. You don't have to *earn* an audience with the King. He is always accessible to you.

A FINAL WORD ON BALANCE

In addition to all the wonderful "positives" we've just covered in this chapter, I feel a need for balance is in order. We are created in God's image—that's truth. We are children of God—that's truth. But it is equally important to understand one last issue:

We are not God.

We don't want to have inflated views of ourselves. Isaiah made this clear in his writings:

> "For my thoughts are not your thoughts,
>   neither are your ways my ways,"
>   declares the LORD.
> "As the heavens are higher than the earth,
>   so are my ways higher than your ways
>   and my thoughts than your thoughts."
>
> Isaiah 55:8–9, NIV

We are not God. We aren't all-knowing, all-powerful, or every-where at once. We sin and have all the problems that come from sin. Paul expressed it this way in Romans:

> For the good that I will to do, I do not do; but the evil I will not to do, that I practice.
>
> Romans 7:19

The bottom line is worth repeating: We need to see ourselves as God sees us. That means seeing the positives—we belong to

God and were created in His image—but it also means facing
the negatives—we are not God's equals and have deficits in our
characters that lead to sin. When that is accomplished, we will
have a balanced, healthy, realistic view of who we really are.

LOOKING OVER
WHERE WE'VE BEEN

We've just examined fourteen different theological truths, re-
vealing who we are from God's perspective. Does any of this truth
really make a difference in your life? I hope you can answer, "It
does make a difference!"

Let's review each of these truths. I've stated each one again in
the space below. After each truth is the word, *therefore*. In other
words, what difference does this truth make to you? For instance,
you may read, "You will never be condemned by God," and you can
write, "Therefore I need never feel rejection from Him."

You Are a Special Creation of God

Therefore: _____

_____

You Are of Infinite Value to God

Therefore: _____

_____

You Have Been Adopted by God

Therefore: _____

_____

You Are a Child of God

Therefore: _____

_____

You Are a Brother or Sister to Jesus

Therefore: _____

_____

You Are a Joint Heir with Christ

Therefore: _____

_____

You Have the Holy Spirit as a Guarantee of Your Inheritance

Therefore: _____

_____

You Have Jesus' Life Within You

Therefore: _____

_____

You Have Jesus' Righteousness

Therefore: _____

_____

You Will Never Be Condemned by God

Therefore: _____

_____

You Are a Foreigner in this World

Therefore: _____

_____

You Have Unique God-Given Abilities

Therefore: _____

_____

You Have a Challenging Vocation

Therefore: _____

_____

You Can Confidently Ask God for Unearned Help

Therefore: _____

_____

GROUP DISCUSSION STARTERS

1. If we are all God's creation, what is the difference between a Christian and a non-Christian from God's perspective?

2. What is the significance of God putting great value on you? How do you personally fight your battles with low self-esteem?

3. How can we dislike ourselves if God has chosen us?

4. What does it mean to you to be called a child of God? Share as personally as you feel comfortable with this group.

5. We often think of ourselves as God's children, but being Jesus' brother or sister may be a new concept to you. First of all, do you agree with the truth, theologically? What are its implications?

6. What thoughts come to mind when you think of God's inheritance?

7. How do you personally experience the Holy Spirit at work inside you? How would you explain it to someone else?

8. What is the difference between the Holy Spirit within you and Christ within you? Are they different or the same? Explain your answer.

9. Is rejection an issue in your life? Can you share a few personal thoughts about it? What does it mean to you to know that there is no condemnation from Christ?

10. How would you communicate to your children the concept of being a foreigner in this world? How can a Christian be *in* the world, but not *of* the world?

11. Are all talents given by God? Is there a difference between a gift and an ability? Do you know what your spiritual gifts are? Share them with the group.

12. From your personal perspective, what are the most important qualities an ambassador of Christ should possess?

13. What has God been doing in your prayer life lately? Are there answers to prayer that you can share with the group?

14. Conclude your session by returning to your buddy for an update on the progress in his or her life. How did the study of this chapter affect him or her this week? What was the most important lesson learned? How can you pray for him or her this week?

Chapter 12

PRESSING ON TO THE MIND OF CHRIST:

$\mathbf{O}$ur study has taken us on a great and wonderful journey. We've covered a lot of ground in discovering the lies that can defeat us and the truths that can bring us to emotional health and spiritual maturity.

During my years as an educator, I became a real believer in the power of *review*. It is a proven method to drive home the truth. I want to use the final chapter of this workbook to walk back through the steps we already traveled on this journey. It is my hope that this review will further implant the importance of the truths we've discussed. Don't be in a hurry. Take your time and allow the material to speak to you once again.

SELF LIES

The first group of lies we looked at were lies we tell ourselves. If we're not careful, they can really get a grip on us emotionally.

Look back through chapter 3 in your workbook. Reflect on what you have learned and the progress you have made.

I Must Be Perfect

Do you struggle with this issue? (Circle one.)

Often   *Sometimes*   *Never*

Write down your struggle. _____

_____

_____

What is the truth? _____

_____

List a biblical reference that supports this truth.

_____

I Must Have Everyone's Love and Approval

Do you struggle with this issue? (Circle one.)

Often   *Sometimes*   *Never*

Write down your struggle. _____

_____

_____

What is the truth? _____

_____

List a biblical reference that supports this truth.

_____

It Is Easier to Avoid Problems Than to Face Them

Do you struggle with this issue? (Circle one.)

       Often   *Sometimes*   *Never*

Write down your struggle. _____

_____

_____

What is the truth? _____

_____

List a biblical reference that supports this truth.

_____

I Can't Be Happy Unless Things Go My Way

Do you struggle with this issue? (Circle one.)

       Often   *Sometimes*   *Never*

Write down your struggle. _____

_____

_____

What is the truth? _____

_____

List a biblical reference that supports this truth.

_____

My Unhappiness Is Somebody Else's Fault

Do you struggle with this issue? (Circle one.)

       Often   *Sometimes*   *Never*

Write down your struggle. _____

_____

_____

What is the truth? _____

_____

List a biblical reference that supports this truth.

_____

WORLDLY LIES

Next we looked at the lies we receive from the world around us. Through advertisements, television shows, movies, magazines, and books, we are bombarded by these messages every day. Review your notes in this chapter, and record your progress below.

You Can Have It All

Do you struggle with this issue? (Circle one.)

       Often   *Sometimes*   *Never*

Write down your struggle. _____

_____

_____

What is the truth? _____

_____

List a biblical reference that supports this truth.

_____

You Are Only as Good as What You Do

Do you struggle with this issue? (Circle one.)

Often   *Sometimes*   *Never*

Write down your struggle. _____

_____

_____

What is the truth? _____

_____

List a biblical reference that supports this truth.

_____

Life Should Be Easy

Do you struggle with this issue? (Circle one.)

Often   *Sometimes*   *Never*

Write down your struggle. _____

_____

_____

What is the truth? _____

_____

List a biblical reference that supports this truth.

_____

Life Should Be Fair

Do you struggle with this issue? (Circle one.)

Often   *Sometimes*   *Never*

Write down your struggle. _____

_____

_____

What is the truth? _____

_____

List a biblical reference that supports this truth.

_____

I Shouldn't Have to Wait for What I Want in Life

Do you struggle with this issue? (Circle one.)

       Often   *Sometimes*   *Never*

Write down your struggle. _____

_____

_____

What is the truth? _____

_____

List a biblical reference that supports this truth.

_____

People Are Basically Good

Do you struggle with this issue? (Circle one.)

       Often   *Sometimes*   *Never*

Write down your struggle. _____

_____

_____

What is the truth? _____

_____

List a biblical reference that supports this truth.

_____

MARITAL LIES

Lies can come into our marriage and cause trouble. We looked at six distortions of the truth that have particular impact on our marital relationship. Review your notes and answer the following questions.

Our Problems Are All Your Fault

Do you struggle with this issue? (Circle one.)

       Often   *Sometimes*   *Never*

Write down your struggle. _____

_____

_____

What is the truth? _____

_____

List a biblical reference that supports this truth.

_____

If It Takes Hard Work, We Must Not Be Right for Each Other

Do you struggle with this issue? (Circle one.)

       Often   *Sometimes*   *Never*

Write down your struggle. _____

_____

_____

What is the truth? _____

_____

List a biblical reference that supports this truth.

_____

You Can and Should Meet All My Needs

Do you struggle with this issue? (Circle one.)

Often   _Sometimes_   _Never_

Write down your struggle. _____

_____

_____

What is the truth? _____

_____

List a biblical reference that supports this truth.

_____

You Owe Me

Do you struggle with this issue? (Circle one.)

Often   _Sometimes_   _Never_

Write down your struggle. _____

_____

_____

What is the truth? _____

_____

List a biblical reference that supports this truth.

_____

I Shouldn't Have to Change

Do you struggle with this issue? (Circle one.)

Often   *Sometimes*   *Never*

Write down your struggle. _____

_____

_____

What is the truth? _____

_____

List a biblical reference that supports this truth.

_____

You Should Be Like Me

Do you struggle with this issue? (Circle one.)

Often   *Sometimes*   *Never*

Write down your struggle. _____

_____

_____

What is the truth? _____

_____

List a biblical reference that supports this truth.

_____

DISTORTION LIES

In our minds, we often distort reality. We examined six distortion lies and offset them with the truth. Did these hit home to you? Jot down your thoughts in the spaces that follow.

Making a Mountain out of a Molehill

What is the truth? _____

_____

How does this lie distort the truth? _____

_____

_____

List a biblical reference that supports this truth.

_____

Taking Everything Personally

What is the truth? _____

_____

How does this lie distort the truth? _____

_____

_____

List a biblical reference that supports this truth.

_____

Seeing Everything as Black/White

What is the truth? _____

_____

How does this lie distort the truth? _____

_____

_____

List a biblical reference that supports this truth.

_____

Missing the Forest for the Trees

What is the truth? _____

_____

How does this lie distort the truth? _____

_____

_____

List a biblical reference that supports this truth.

_____

History Always Repeats Itself

What is the truth? _____

_____

How does this lie distort the truth? _____

_____

_____

List a biblical reference that supports this truth.

_____

Don't Confuse Me with the Facts

What is the truth? _____

_____

How does this lie distort the truth? _____

_____

_____

_____

List a biblical reference that supports this truth.

_____

RELIGIOUS LIES

Sometimes in our religious training we are taught erroneous concepts of God, ourselves, and life. If we don't catch them, they can stay with us and haunt us to the point of wrecking our lives. If we misinterpret what the Bible teaches, we can end up believing lies that destroy us. Review your notes then work the following exercise.

God's Love Must Be Earned

Do you struggle with this issue? (Circle one.)

        Often   _Sometimes_   _Never_

Write down your struggle. _____

_____

_____

What is the truth? _____

_____

What does the Bible teach about this truth? _____

_____

God Hates the Sin and the Sinner

Do you struggle with this issue? (Circle one.)

        Often   _Sometimes_   _Never_

Write down your struggle. _____

_____

_____

What is the truth? _____

_____

What does the Bible teach about this truth? _____

_____

Because I'm a Christian, God Will Protect Me from Pain and Suffering

Do you struggle with this issue? (Circle one.)

        Often   *Sometimes*   *Never*

Write down your struggle. _____

_____

_____

What is the truth? _____

_____

What does the Bible teach about this truth? _____

_____

All My Problems Are Caused by My Sins

Do you struggle with this issue? (Circle one.)

        Often   *Sometimes*   *Never*

Write down your struggle. _____

_____

_____

What is the truth? _____

_____

What does the Bible teach about this truth? _____

_____

It Is My Christian Duty to Meet All the Needs of Others

Do you struggle with this issue? (Circle one.)

      Often   *Sometimes*   *Never*

Write down your struggle. _____

_____

_____

What is the truth? _____

_____

What does the Bible teach about this truth? _____

_____

A Good Christian Doesn't Feel Angry, Anxious, or Depressed

Do you struggle with this issue? (Circle one.)

      Often   *Sometimes*   *Never*

Write down your struggle. _____

_____

_____

What is the truth? _____

_____

What does the Bible teach about this truth? _____

_____

God Can't Use Me Unless I'm Spiritually Strong

Do you struggle with this issue? (Circle one.)

          Often   *Sometimes*   *Never*

Write down your struggle. _____

_____

_____

What is the truth? _____

_____

What does the Bible teach about this truth? _____

_____

THE TRUTHS FOR EMOTIONAL HEALTH

In chapters 8 and 9, we looked at twelve critically important truths for living an emotionally healthy life. Review these truths and reflect on what you learned. I hope you will be encouraged by all the progress you've made through interacting with all this material!

To Err Is Human

Why is this an important truth to you? _____

_____

What is the distortion of this truth? _____

_____

What Bible verse reinforces this truth?

_____

How can you apply this truth to your life? _____

_____

_____

What "Should" Have Happened Did

Why is this an important truth to you? _____

_____

What is the distortion of this truth? _____

_____

What Bible verse reinforces this truth?

_____

How can you apply this truth to your life? _____

_____

_____

You Can't Please Everyone

Why is this an important truth to you? _____

_____

What is the distortion of this truth? _____

_____

What Bible verse reinforces this truth?

_____

How can you apply this truth to your life? _____

_____

You Don't Have To

Why is this an important truth to you? _____

_____

What is the distortion of this truth? _____

_____

What Bible verse reinforces this truth?

_____

How can you apply this truth to your life? _____

_____

_____

You Are Going to Die

Why is this an important truth to you? _____

_____

What is the distortion of this truth? _____

_____

What Bible verse reinforces this truth?

_____

How can you apply this truth to your life? _____

_____

_____

The Virtue Lies in the Struggle, Not the Prize

Why is this an important truth to you? _____

_____

What is the distortion of this truth? _____

_____

What Bible verse reinforces this truth?

_____

How can you apply this truth to your life? _____

_____

_____

You Are Not Entitled

Did you believe this truth before our study? (Circle one.)

      No   *Somewhat*   *Yes*

What was the most helpful lesson your learned from this section?

_____

_____

What does the Bible teach about this truth? _____

_____

What can you do to put this truth into practice? _____

_____

_____

There Is No Gain Without Pain

Did you believe this truth before our study? (Circle one.)

      No   *Somewhat*   *Yes*

What was the most helpful lesson your learned from this section?

_____

_____

What does the Bible teach about this truth? _____

_____

What can you do to put this truth into practice? _____

_____

_____

Your Childhood Isn't Over

Did you believe this truth before our study? (Circle one.)

     No   *Somewhat*   *Yes*

What was the most helpful lesson your learned from this section?

_____

_____

What does the Bible teach about this truth? _____

_____

What can you do to put this truth into practice? _____

_____

_____

Emotional Problems Are Good

Did you believe this truth before our study? (Circle one.)

     No   *Somewhat*   *Yes*

What was the most helpful lesson your learned from this section?

_____

_____

What does the Bible teach about this truth? _____

_____

What can you do to put this truth into practice? _____
_____
_____

You Reap What You Sow

Did you believe this truth before our study? (Circle one.)

        No   *Somewhat*   *Yes*

What was the most helpful lesson your learned from this section?
_____
_____

What does the Bible teach about this truth? _____
_____

What can you do to put this truth into practice? _____
_____
_____

Life Is Difficult

Did you believe this truth before our study? (Circle one.)

        No   *Somewhat*   *Yes*

What was the most helpful lesson your learned from this section?
_____
_____

What does the Bible teach about this truth? _____
_____

What can you do to put this truth into practice? _____
_____
_____

A FINAL WORD

Congratulations! Completing this workbook is a major accomplishment. I want you to be encouraged as a result of this study. One of the most encouraging aspects of this workbook is that you can take its application with you everywhere you go. You can continue to overcome the lies that plague you. How?

Keep using the truth.

Remember the Scriptures that we worked through.

Use the TRUTH system as your guide past the lies that harm you to the truths that can set you free.

Now that you know how to practically apply the "mind of Christ" in daily situations, press on!

Emotional health and spiritual maturity can be yours. Go for it!

GROUP DISCUSSION STARTERS

1. Use the final session as a time of reflection. Have group members share their thoughts on the following:

- What was the most meaningful truth you discovered in this study?
- Share something you did not know before this study, that you came to know as a result of your time together.
- If you're comfortable in doing so, share the most painful issue you encountered in this workbook. How did you deal with it once you uncovered it?
- What was the greatest lesson you learned about emotional health?
- What was the most significant spiritual lesson you learned?
- How will you apply the TRUTH system in your everyday life?

- What does it mean to you to develop the "mind of Christ" in your practical world?
- If there was one thing you could pass on from this workbook, what would it be?

2. Spend a few minutes with your buddy. Think back through all you two have shared. Take a few minutes to pray together. Thank God for the benefits you two have experienced together. End your time by arranging to keep in touch periodically.